BURGERS TO BANQUETS

THE
BARBECUE
BOOK

Jim Marks
('Mr Barbecue')

Kitbridge
Publishing Ltd

First published in Great Britain in 2001 by
Kitbridge Publishing Ltd.
In association with Outback UK.

Photographs on cover and pages 7 *(fish picture)*, 71, 86 *(Stir-fried
chicken)*, 112, 121, 126 *(Gateau paysanne)*, 137 *(Foccacia)*, by **Paul
Dixon Photography**, Hollingbourne, Kent. All other photographs by
Geoff Stanton Photography, Stoke Goldington, Bucks.

Design and illustrations: **Impact-IM Ltd**, Farleigh Bridge, Maidstone, Kent.
Food preparation for photography: Jim Marks and Angela Dixon.
Printed and bound in Great Britain by **Fulmar Colour Printing
Corporation Ltd**, Croydon.

ISBN   0 9531962 1 6

Notes on recipes
Ingredients are given in both metric and imperial measures. Use either
set of quantities, but not a mixture of both, in any one recipe.
All spoon measurements are level unless otherwise stated.
1 tablespoon = one 15ml spoon
1 teaspoon = one 5ml spoon
Eggs are standard (size 3) unless otherwise stated.

Kitbridge Publishing Limited
Pear Tree Cottage, Chardstock,
Nr Axminster, Devon, EX13 7BN.

contents

Pictured opposite:
Crown of roast lamb (page 48)

acknowledgements

The first vote of thanks goes to the team at Impact IM. Glyn Roberts, for creating the book's attractive cover design, graphics and illustrations, Alison Whittingham for expertly transmitting my copy to the printed page and Tim Smith for master-minding the whole project. Talking of creativity, I would like to salute those talented photographers, Paul Dixon and Geoff Stanton, whose work illuminates the book. I leave it for you to decide which of the dishes, photographed by them, had been cooked on charcoal-burning units and which were cooked on gas barbecues (it's roughly a 50/50 split). Talking of food, I owe a debt of gratitude to Angela Dixon for being such a terrific helpmate in the food preparation department, even though she was busily engaged with her photographic duties. Many thanks also to Eric Hopper and Julie Channer of Outback UK for kindly letting me borrow several different models from their company's super range of barbecues to cook on.

The excellent selection of meat, some of which is featured on the front cover, was obtained from 'Complete Meats of Axminster', one of the UK's top family butchers. Whilst handing out the kudos, I would like to express my gratitude to Simon Cross for his kind help and expert advice in printing matters. I would also like to take this opportunity to warmly thank celebrity chefs Brian Turner, Ross Burden and Ainsley Harriot (barbecue cooking virtuosos all) for their noble work in helping to advance the cause of barbecuing in Great Britain, and likewise fellow-enthusiasts and friends, Graham Ducker and Martin Cobban. The final words of thanks must however go to the millions of barbecue aficionados for their selfless support of breweries, wine producers, farmers, butchers, fishermen, fishmongers, vegetable and fruit growers, grocers, makers of sauces (soy, tomato and stir-fry), oil (olive, vegetable, groundnut, Worcestershire etc), manufacturers of kitchen towelling, foil, burn lotion, barbecues, barbecue accessories, to mention just a few, and, lastly, the authors of barbecue cook-books.

Who knows when, where and by whom, the first piece of meat was cooked over hot coals, but like most great discoveries it probably came about from a happy combination of accident and chance. Tracing outdoor, or 'in cave' cooking to its pre-historic roots is impossible, but archaeologists have unearthed ample evidence that man has been perfecting his open-fire cooking techniques for thousands of years. As far as pictorial evidence of early forms of barbecues is concerned, the famous Bayeux Tapestry depicts a farewell party, held by Odo, Bishop of Bayeux, in honour of his liege lord William Duke of Normandy, just prior to William and his army setting off across the Channel in 1066. The relevant panels show busy servants offering the guests a generous selection of kebabs, sausages and spit-roast chickens, all cooked it would appear, on the French equivalent of open barbecues. Despite my misgivings, I must support the hypothesis that this hearty consumption of barbecue fare by William and his men had a direct, some might say unfair, bearing on the outcome of William's forthcoming engagement at Hastings.

The modern barbecue phenomenon probably took root in the British colony of Virginia in the latter part of the 17th century, when the settlers embarked on the practise of holding large social gatherings centred on outdoor cooking feasts. As far as the word 'barbecue' itself is concerned, my vote goes to the theory that it is a bastard form of 'barbe a queue' ('whiskers to tail'), a phrase reputedly used by French settlers in Louisiana to characterize spit-roasting a whole animal.

For me there is no mystery as to why barbecuing has developed into such a hugely popular world-wide pastime. It is the almost magical combination of fire, food, family, friends and fun that does the trick. What other social pursuit produces so much pleasure, with so little effort and cost?

As you will, hopefully, deduce from the recipes on the following pages, one can tackle virtually any type of food on a barbecue and cater for most tastes and occasions, be it breakfast, lunch, a sophisticated dinner or large scale party. I have enjoyed barbecuing on the beach, on balconies, on board boats, in car parks, in TV and Radio studios, on the river bank and on patios etc. For a growing number of aficionados, barbecue time is any time and, if the weather is somewhat inclement, (which on odd occasions it is) one can, with a covered barbecue, cook out and eat in. So anyone owning a lidded barbecue who doesn't press it into service on Christmas Day, regardless of snow or rain, is wasting a golden opportunity to conjure up a truly magnificent turkey, perhaps a joint of beef, whilst at the same time liberating stacks of valuable (and pristine!) oven space.

Always keep in mind the saying 'The food you cook on a barbecue which looks darn good and smells darn good, will taste darn good and do you and yours the power of good!'

Happy barbecuing

Jim Marks

foreword

In the comparatively short time I have known Jim Marks, I have learnt two major facts. The first is that Jim can talk like nobody else that I know, and secondly that when I want to know anything about the art of barbecuing, then he's the man.

I live my life cooking and talking about food and drink, and this has always been the love of my life. Now I've discovered barbecuing and fallen in love again, with the art and not Jim, I hasten to add.

So suddenly life is great and all I need to know is here in this book, it's wonderful, aren't I lucky. Wherever you sit on the 'Richter' scale of barbecuing this book is for you - enjoy.

Brian J. Turner

Chef/Restaurateur

Pictured opposite:
Soy-glazed roast loin of pork (page 67)
Daily bread with Cheese and herb rolls (page 139)
Hickory smoked turkey with Scottish glaze (page 89)

cookingtechniques

Apart from 'Smoke-cooking', 'Baking' and 'Vegetables in foil', the various barbecue cooking techniques, described below, have been divided into two segments. The first segment relates to the use of charcoal/wood burning barbecues and the second relates to the use of gas barbecues.

Open grill cooking

Open grill cooking, Direct cooking or just plain Grilling, all mean the same thing, cooking food directly over radiant heat
– from whatever its source. Grilling is the most popular and widely practised of all the barbecue cooking techniques and for many people, it is synonymous with 'barbecuing', which is hardly surprising bearing in mind that the word, and the activity, have been so closely related for several hundred years.

Grilling is a cooking technique that requires the cook's constant attention, so anything that can be cooked fairly quickly, 30 minutes or less, is a suitable candidate for this method eg. steaks, chops, chicken and turkey portions, hamburgers, sausages, kebabs, whole fish and fish steaks. One exception would be *Butterflied leg of lamb* (recipe on page 47) where the grilling time could be in the order of 35-50 minutes depending on the weight and thickness of the joint.

There is a broad guide to grilling times on page 185, but always bear in mind that air temperature and wind strength, can have a marked effect on the cooking times quoted. However, for those owners of covered barbecues intent on barbecuing some steaks, regardless of how awful the weather is, all they have to do is to carry on cooking with the lid in position. A considerable volume of smoke will be produced, but as much of it will be trapped under the lid, this will only add additional 'je ne sais quoi' to the steaks appearance and flavour.

Grilling

Using charcoal-burning barbecues

1. Start your fire, following the instructions set out on page 174. Wait until most of the charcoal is covered in grey ash before starting to cook.

2. Prior to placing the grill on the barbecue, brush the grill bars over with cooking oil to lubricate them, or perhaps rub with some of the fat that has been trimmed from the meat.

3. If the barbecue design allows, adjust the level of the food grill to about 8cm (3-4 inches) above the fire-bed. Cooking at this level for a minute or so will sear the surface of the meat, thereby locking in those valuable juices which make such a valuable contribution to the meat's succulence.

Using gas barbecues

1. Remove the food grill(s) before lighting the gas and brush over with cooking oil to lubricate. If some fat has been trimmed from the meat, you could, alternatively, use this as a natural lubricant.

2. With the lid open, ignite the gas burners at the 'High heat' setting. Close the lid and allow the barbecue's fire-bed (volcanic rock etc) to reach grilling heat – this should take 5-10 minutes depending on the state of the weather and the barbecue model.

2. Replace the food grills just prior to the commencement of cooking.

3. Adjust the gas control knobs to the required setting (more on this follows).

4. Position the food on the grill(s). Avoid crowding the grill surface, especially with fatty foods such as sausages, hamburgers, chicken pieces etc.

5. As a general rule, select a low to medium heat setting when tackling fish, vegetables and fruit and a medium heat when dealing with beef, pork, lamb and poultry. Apart

from pre-heating, and helping to clean, the barbecue, the 'High heat' setting may be used occasionally for searing steaks etc but, culinary speaking, for very little else.

General hint on grilling

▍ If you are using a thick basting sauce – containing sugar, jam, honey or ketchup - brush it on during the final few minutes of cooking. If applied too early, especially at high cooking temperatures, the surface of the meat will quickly burn and char.

▍ Grill one side of the meat for the time recommended in the recipe or cooking time chart. Brush the uncooked surface with oil or butter. Turn the meat over and complete the cooking cycle.

▍ Meat marinated for a few hours, or overnight in the refrigerator, moistens, flavours and tenderises the meat. A cheaper lean cut, such as chuck, will benefit from an oil-based marinade.

▍ Use long-handled tongs, with 'soft jaws', to turn steaks. Tongs that have sharp teeth may pierce the meat and accidentally cause the loss of precious juices.

▍ Thaw frozen meat whilst it marinates. Simply keep the meat in the marinade, turning it a few times, if it is not completely immersed.

Grilling Kebabs

For sheer versatility, skewer-cooking takes some beating! It alone gives the cook a completely free rein to produce a boundless variety of food with which to please the partialities and palates of all and sundry. Meat, poultry, fish, vegetables and fruit can all be cooked on a skewer, separately or in eye-catching, mouth-watering, combinations where the intermingling juices blend together to generate delicious new taste sensations.

If necessary, the taste and tenderness of the kebabs can be further enhanced by marinating the food with wine, herbs, spices etc.

▍ Oiling metal skewers, prior to threading on chunks of meat and fish, will help to pre-vent the food from sticking. Bamboo skewers, traditionally used for satay, should be soaked in water before use, in order to reduce the chances of them burning during cooking.

▍ When cutting up chunks of fish for impaling on a skewer, leaving the skin of the fish on will help to hold the flesh together whilst it is being pierced and later, whilst it is being cooked.

▍ Composing the contents of a skewer with food of roughly similar cooking span will help to produce balanced results. Alternatively, part-cooking the slower cooking food, prior to making up the complete skewer, will help to even out the disparity. ie. for mixed vegetable kebabs, parboiling the harder, slower cooking, items, such as corn on the cob, small onions and potatoes, will help to even out cooking times.

▍ Use the warming grill (rack) of your barbecue to support and gently cook all-vegetable kebabs whilst in the process of cooking meat on the grill below. Finishing off the vegetables on the main grill will give them some attractive sear marks to match those of the meat.

▍ Trim excess fat from meat to help reduce potential flare-ups (turn to page 176 for some helpful hints on how to avoid flare-ups).

▍ Finally, try not to 'log-jam' the skewer with food – particularly meat. Leave small gaps so that the heat can get through to all surfaces.

'Indirect heat' cooking

As mentioned above, it is possible and very practical – particularly when the weather has turned 'beastly',– to use a covered barbecue for fast-cooking food such as steaks, chops and hamburgers, but to extract the maximum benefit from your investment in a covered unit, it should be regularly pressed into service to roast joints, whole birds and thick slabs of meat. If you do not, it could perhaps be regarded as tantamount to driving your new, dream, sports car, half a mile to the village Post Office – once a week! You should in fact give serious consideration to treating your covered barbecue as a trusted deputy to its kitchen-bound sidekick, and employ it at every opportunity throughout the spring and summer. One has to bear in mind that apart from turning out superb roasts, a covered barbecue is quite capable of being used to bake anything from bread to apple pies (more on this below).

Summer-time is obviously the peak barbecue period, but come Christmas Day, a golden opportunity arises to summon your mothballed barbecue from the back of the garage in order to relieve the considerable pressure the day brings on the kitchen oven (not to mention the hard-pressed cook and washing-up brigade). More, on this charitable opportunity, on page 88.

Roasting

With charcoal-burning barbecues

Start the fire, following the instructions on page 175. Place the joint on the grill directly over the pan. With the lid in position, the heat from the fire-bed will reflect off the lid to roast the joint *a la* your kitchen oven.

With gas barbecues

Place a drip pan, under the food grill, to one side of the barbecue for two burner units or in the centre of the grill for 3-4 burner units. Ideally the pan should be large enough to catch all the fats falling away from the food set on the grill above, but not so large that its bulk intrudes into the barbecue's lit-burner area.

With the lid in the open position, ignite the gas burner, using the 'High heat' setting, adjacent (not under) to where the drip pan is sitting.

Close the lid and leave the barbecue alone for 5-10 minutes.

Having placed the food on the grill immediately above the drip pan, re-close the lid.

Adjust the temperature setting as required (the 'Medium' heat setting should be adequate for most dishes). If intending to place the food on the barbecue immediately upon ignition, do remember to adjust the heat setting to the required level as soon as the warm-up period has been completed.

Baking

Imagine - a magnificent roast chicken has just been removed from the barbecue to rest and allow its juices to settle down, before it is carved and served up to the hungry horde. Waiting quietly in the wings to take its place, is an unbaked apple pie or, better still, a bread and butter pudding. By now, the heat from the fire-bed is likely to be in an ideal state to bake the pie or the pudding so, having placed the desert in the spot previously occupied by the chicken, the lid is replaced and the barbecue left to carry on baking. Some 30 or 40 minutes later, the lid of the barbecue is removed to reveal a truly scrumptious dish which, although 'barbecue – baked', will certainly not have inherited a barbecue flavour! Bread that has been baked under the lid of a covered barbecue always looks well and tastes well, with Ciabatta being a personal favourite. A pizza, hot and bubbling off the barbecue, is a fairly close match (visually at least) to one that has been prepared in a Tuscan pizzeria.

Baking procedure

If planning to bake something from scratch, simply follow the roasting directions set out above. You may, if you wish to, omit the drip pan with the proviso that by so doing the charcoal fire-bed is not allowed to inch its way towards the centre of the grate.

Smoke-cooking
With charcoal or gas barbecues

Do not confuse 'smoke-cooking' with 'smoking' (smoke-curing). 'Smoking' is a slow, highly skilled process, the primary aim being to preserve the meat and fish. This will require a working temperature as low as 10°C/50°F and can take several days to complete. 'Smoke-cooking', on the other hand, is a 'hot' process, carried out at normal oven temperatures. The exception being the 'barbecue smokers', referred to on page 163, which operate in the 80-100°C range. Whilst contributing very little to the food, preservation-wise, smoke-cooking undoubtedly helps to give meat and poultry, in particular, a richer, deeper colour, and a more piquant flavour, than food which has been roasted in the normal manner. .

One can 'smoke-cook' food in any charcoal or gas-fired covered barbecue - the cooking times being similar to regular barbecuing. Apart from ham, poultry, pork (including spare-ribs), lamb, venison, kidneys and sausages, a wide variety of fish and shellfish – such as trout, mackerel, salmon, eel and oysters, are all excellent fare for this highly satisfying barbecue cooking technique.

Aromatic smoking woods such as hickory (the most popular), oak and mesquite are available from barbecue stockists. Indigenous hardwoods suitable for 'hot-smoking' include cherry, apple, beech, alder, sycamore and poplar. Vine cuttings are excellent for smoke-cooking but do have a rather limited burn-period. *Do not, however, be tempted to use pine, or other resinous wood,* as doing so will impart an unpleasant taste to the food. The natural fragrance of the selected smoking-wood can, if desired, be masked, perhaps enhanced, by adding some rosemary or thyme sprigs to the fire-bed.

The selected smoking-wood, or commercial wood and herb mixtures, should be well soaked with water before adding to the coals. Experience will tell you how much wood to use, and when it should be added to the fire-bed. For your first attempt, try adding two handfuls of wood chips, or a fist-sized chunk of wood, to the fire-bed about half way through roasting a chicken. This should be sufficient to transform the skin of the bird to an attractive 'golden/mahogany' colour and give the flesh of the bird a delicate smoky flavour. The next time you set out to smoke-cook a chicken, you can vary the amount of wood, and the time it is applied, to give the bird more, or less, colour and flavour to suit your taste.

If you have a penchant for 'smoky-barbecue' flavoured baked beans, try leaving an open pot of beans (I use an old Spanish earthenware pot) alongside the meat during the last 20 minutes or so of smoke-cooking a chicken etc. Stir the beans occasionally to prevent the top layer from drying out and crusting up too much.

▋ Brushing a glaze over the surface of a smoke-cooked joint will add a lovely sheen to the joint's handsome exterior. Do not brush the glaze on too early or it will caramelise and burn – 10 to15 minutes before the end of cooking should be OK but do keep an eye on the food.

▋ Small wood chips tend to burn away quite quickly. 'Bundle-wrapping'* the water-soaked chips in a couple of layers of foil will help to extend their smoking-life. Having made a series of small holes in the package, to allow the resultant smoke to escape, place the package on the food grill or directly onto the fire-bed.

*Refer to 'Vegetables in foil' (page 15) for further details.

Spit-roasting

Watching a leg of lamb, loin of pork, chicken or turkey, slowly revolving on a spit, whilst relaxing in your garden chair, quaffing a glass of wine, beer etc, is peculiarly satisfying – indeed for some, it is the culinary equivalent of watching men digging a hole in the road. Small wonder then, that certain catering establishments, in-store delicatessens etc, use a multiple spit-roaster as a powerful magnet with which to attract the punter's attention.

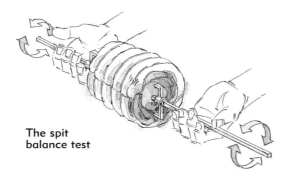

The spit balance test

Using charcoal-burning barbecues

Apart from small portable units, the majority of charcoal barbecues, be they 'Wagon' or 'Brazier' models, will allow the user to install a spit-roast assembly (spits, spit motors and spit accessories are covered on page 170).

The procedure

Prepare the fire-bed for spit-roasting (see page 175). Having made sure that the prongs on the lower set of tines are facing away from the handle, pass the spit rod through the centre of the food. In order for the roast to rotate smoothly, it must be evenly balanced on the spit rod. A poorly balanced joint, or bird, will rotate in fits and starts. As a result, there will be excessive wear on the spit motor.

To check that the food on the spit is evenly balanced; rotate the laden spit slowly across the palm of your hands (see drawing). Should there be little or no tendency for food to roll suddenly from any position, the balance will be good. In the case of a jerky roll, re-skewer the food to correct the imbalance. With a little practice, you should be able to pass the spit rod through the centre of the food's mass regardless of its shape.

When preparing a leg of lamb or leg of pork for spit-roasting, insert the spit into the leg at the fillet end (next to the knuckle of the leg bone). Having carefully pushed the spit through the leg to run alongside the bone, push one of the prongs from the second set of tines, into the narrow shank end of the leg. If spit-roasting a rib roast, shoulder, or loin, of pork, beef or lamb, insert the spit near the bones at one corner of the joint and push diagonally through the meat until it emerges close to the opposite corner. If spit-roasting poultry or game birds, very carefully push the tip of the spit through the 'parson's nose', into the body cavity and out through the flap of skin at the bird's neck. Having firmly secured the tines, use string to tie the bird into a compact shape.

Try to obtain a steel pan that is narrow in width and fairly shallow in depth. Fill about three quarters of the drip pan with water or, if you intend using the fat-enriched liquid as a savoury baste, with beer or wine to which a few herbs can be added if you wish.

Position the food-laden spit, and adjust the spit-motor so that the food rotates up and away from you. The fats and juices should fall directly into the drip pan – if not, adjust the pan's position accordingly.

Using a gas barbecue

A spit-roast assembly (rotisserie) can be fitted to most 'Wagon' gas barbecues - a few models have them as a standard accessory and one or two come with a rotisserie burner which, unusually, is fitted at the rear of its lower housing. The largest gas 'Wagons' have correspondingly deep lids and burner housings that enable them, with the lid closed, to accommodate a spitted turkey or joint weighing in the region of 9kg (20 lb). Although not a technique that will excite avid 'spit-watchers' (referred to above), spit-roasting, with the lid down, is a lot more energy efficient than spit-roasting carried out on an open barbecue.

The procedure

Remove the food grills and place a steel drip pan (an aluminium pan can be used if your barbecue has a rear mounted burner) directly on the fire-bed, parallel to, and slightly in front of where the spit will sit. As mentioned above, try to obtain a pan that is narrow in width and fairly shallow in depth – especially if there is relatively little space between the top of the fire-bed and the spit-rod. Again, fill about three quarters of the pan with water or with a cocktail of water, beer or wine.

With the lid open, ignite the burners at the 'High heat' setting. Close the lid and leave for 5-10 minutes.

Having adjusted the temperature-setting (I suggest somewhere in the region of low to medium), place the food-laden spit in position and adjust the spit-motor so that the food rotates up and away from you. You may have to slightly adjust the location of the pan to ensure that the fats fall directly into it.

- Unless previously marinated, brush the food with oil at the outset of cooking. Periodically baste joints with some of the liquid from the drip pan.

- If impaling more than one piece of meat on the spit, leave a little space between them to allow the heat to reach all surfaces.

- Periodically, check the level of liquid in the drip pan. It will require topping up now and then, but **never** pour water into a drip pan where all, or almost all, the liquid has evaporated.

- If you can obtain a rack of spare ribs from your butcher, try spit-roasting them, or failing that, grilling them. Whilst individual ribs might get tucked into a little sooner, the meat in a rib from a rack, is a little more succulent, and there is more of it to get your teeth into. Prior to threading the ribs, concertina fashion, onto the spit, trim off any excess fat and strip off any membrane. Having cooked the ribs, basting occasionally with a sauce of your choice, ('Rich Chinese sauce'- you will find the recipe on page 158 - is quite yummy) it is very easy to slice the rack into individual ribs.

cooking techniques

Wok-cooking

Cooking with a wok on your barbecue is a fast, healthy, fun way to prepare a wide array of food at a surprisingly modest cost. It will, I promise, give you great cachet with family and friends.

When the wok first came into play, and eventually into general use, is unrecorded, but this 'round-bottomed frying pan' (wok is the Cantonese word for pan) has been the keystone of the Chinese kitchen for the past 5000 years or so. The wok has no peer when it comes to cooking versatility. Whilst most people are familiar with 'quick stir-frying' (some stir-fry recipes are featured on the following pages), relatively few are aware that the wok is equally adept at 'steaming', braising, deep-frying and shallow-frying.

It is quite likely that you already own a wok. If so, check to see if your barbecue will permit the wok to be seated directly on, or very close to, the unit's fire-bed. Unfortunately the shape and size of many charcoal-burning barbecues preclude them from accepting a standard-size domestic wok of about 36cm (14 inches) in diameter. 'Kettles' and open-top 'Brazier' charcoal barbecues are the best bet and the largest models in this category will probably accommodate a larger wok (the larger the wok the better).

Advice on preparing a charcoal fire-bed for wok-cooking is set out on page 174.

Wok-cooking with a gas barbecue

Gas barbecues, particularly those models that have 'side-burners', are eminently suitable for wok-cooking. In 'quick stir-frying', what is obviously needed is speed of cooking and, consequently, 'instant' heat, ie. the ability to turn the heat instantly up when required, as well as instantly down. In this particular respect, a gas barbecue has the edge on a charcoal-burning barbecue.

As a rule, the larger the barbecue and the greater its BTU/kilowatt rating, the better.

The procedure

If your gas barbecue has a side-burner, ignite the burner at full heat and place the wok squarely on the burner's trivet. Should the wok be one-handled, with a round bottom, a trivet stand will help to keep the wok stable during cooking. Adjust the burner control knob to the required setting.

If your gas barbecue does not have a side burner, start by removing the food grills. Ignite the burners at the 'High heat' setting, close the lid (if it is a covered unit) and leave for 5-10 minutes. Position the wok on the fire-bed, adjust the burners to the required heat and start cooking.

- Removing the fire-bed (layer of volcanic rock or ceramic briquettes) from your gas barbecue before ignition, will allow the wok's bottom to be that little bit closer to the burners, thus effectively increasing the wok's work rate.

- Wrapping two or three layers of foil around the bottom of the wok's handle will help to prevent the wood being scorched by the heat rising from the burners.

Stir-frying hints

- Always heat the wok over high heat, for a minute or so, before adding the oil.

- Prior to placing any food in the wok, turn the wok so that its surface is coated with oil. Dry patches on the surface of the wok could result in food sticking, and then burning.

- Make sure your ingredients are completely dry before adding them to the hot oil. Food with excess moisture, when placed in hot oil could cause the oil to splatter.

- Cook the recipe ingredients in the recommended order ie. spring onions, garlic and ginger should be done first. Vegetables and meat should be cooked separately with the hardest vegetables, such as carrot and celery, being tackled before softer items, such as peppers, with bean sprouts and mushrooms last into the wok.

- Unless the recipe indicates otherwise, use high heat when stir-frying and always turn the contents of the wok from the bottom upwards.

- Before cooking shellfish, place a small chunk of fresh root ginger in the hot oil, and leaving for 30 seconds or so. This should slightly mask the fishy aroma and enhance the flavour.

- When you have finished cooking, with the burner still lit, add some hot water to the wok and rub over with a mildly abrasive scouring pad until the wok is clean. Having poured out the water, wipe over with a clean cloth and finish drying off over the heat.

Vegetables in foil

The majority of vegetables take very kindly to being grilled on a barbecue over moderate heat, as indeed they undoubtedly do when stir-fried.

A healthy alternative, although the results are somewhat bland, is to wrap portions of prepared vegetables in foil and 'steam-cook' them. Cooking vegetables in this manner has its benefits:

1. the vegetables retain more of their natural colour

2. the vegetables retain more of their natural flavour and vitamins than when pot-boiled

3. there is no cleaning of pots and pans!!

The procedure

Use 'heavy-duty' (extra thick) aluminium foil for wrapping the vegetables. If only thin foil is available, use two or three layers.

I suggest that packs are limited in size so that they can be more easily tucked in around a joint that is being cooked by 'Indirect heat'. Two to three average portions can be wrapped in a piece of foil roughly 30cm (12 inches) square.

Having cleaned and prepared the vegetables (leave them wet), place in the centre of the foil. Lift the four edges of the foil and add some water, 1 or two tablespoons should be sufficient. If you prefer, add a knob of butter (plain or flavoured), or margarine, in lieu of water.

The wrapping method you employ depends on the cooking technique you intend following. If using 'Indirect heat', I suggest you *bundle-wrap* the vegetables. This will require bringing the four corners of the foil square together to form a rough pyramid shape. Carefully fold the open edges together trying not to crush the package. Keep the package in the upright position.

If it is your intention to cook the vegetables over 'Direct heat', this entails making the package as leak proof as possible bearing in mind that it will be turned over fairly frequently. This will therefore require the vegetables to be *drugstore wrapped*. This will entail placing the vegetables in the centre of a square or oblong piece of heavy-duty foil, or two or three layers of thin foil. Having added water bring the two opposite sides together and turn down the edges in a couple of tight folds ensuring that adequate space is left above the vegetables to allow for heat expansion. Sealing the open ends of the package with a further couple of tight folds will give you a neat, watertight, package.

Barbecued beef morsels

Makes about 40

1kg (2 lb) sirloin of beef,
cut into bite-size pieces

Marinade:

5cm (2 inch) piece of fresh root ginger

2 small onions, chopped

$^1/_2$ teaspoon minced garlic

125g (4oz) sugar

6 small dried chilli peppers or
1 teaspoon chilli powder

2 tablespoons red wine vinegar

4 teaspoons cornflour

To make the marinade, mix the ingredients in a small pan and heat for about 20 minutes or until slightly thick. Blend the cornflour with 150ml of water. Gradually add to the pan and keep stirring until the mixture is clear. Pour the marinade through a wire strainer into a bowl, pressing out all the juices. Discard the pulp and allow the marinade to cool.

Add the beef to the marinade in the bowl, cover and allow to stand for 4-6 hours.

Prepare the barbecue for grilling, following the instructions on page 8.

Thread two to three pieces of meat onto each skewer and grill over medium to high heat, turning and basting frequently with the remaining marinade, for about 10 minutes or cooked to the desired degree.

Olive bacon titbits

Makes 24

12 slices of streaky bacon
24 large green olives, stoned

Soak bamboo skewers or wooden cocktail sticks in water, if using. Prepare the barbecue for grilling following the instructions on page 8.

Cut the bacon slices in half and grill until partially cooked but still flexible. Wrap each olive in a piece of bacon and thread it on to a fine metal or bamboo skewer. Alternatively, secure each bacon-wrapped olive with a wooden cocktail stick.

Grill over medium to high heat for about 10 minutes or until the bacon is crisp and nicely browned. Turn the titbits occasionally during cooking.

Pictured opposite:
Spicy cheesy potato slices
Chicken wings with honey glaze
Spicy grilled prawns

appetisers

Crispy-griddled aubergine wedges

Makes approximately 8-12

2 medium-size aubergines
salt
75g (3oz) plain flour
25g (1oz) cornflour
25g (1oz) butter
1 tablespoon groundnut oil

Peel the aubergines (I find a thin-bladed sharp, serrated, knife is best for this task) and cut into quarters lengthwise. If the aubergines are large, cut into 5 or 6 segments. Place the wedges, cut sides up, on a diner plate and sprinkle over with salt. Sit another diner plate on the aubergine and weigh down with something heavy. Let stand for 30-40 minutes before giving the wedges a thorough rinse under cold running water. Pat dry with kitchen paper.

Prepare the barbecue for grilling, following the instructions on page 8.

Blend the flours together in a bowl. Toss the wedges in the flour to coat them all over, shaking off excess flour.

If the barbecue has a griddle-plate, allow it to get hot before melting the oil and butter together. Otherwise use a heavy-based frying pan or skillet placed directly on the barbecue grill to heat the oil and butter. Cook the wedges for about 2 minutes on each side until nicely browned and crisp all over. Serve immediately as they will tend to 'deflate' if left overlong.

See serving suggestion.

Serving suggestion:
Make up a dip by blending, either 2 teaspoons of hot curry powder (or 1 tablespoon of curry paste) OR 1 teaspoon of Dijon mustard, plus 1 tablespoon tarragon (or Balsamic) vinegar, into 150ml ($^1/_4$ pint) of mayonnaise (recipe page 150).

I suggest the flavouring ingredients are initially added in smaller amounts until you find the taste that suits.

Popcorn

3 tablespoons popping corn
1 tablespoon vegetable oil

Prepare the barbecue for grilling, following the instructions on page 8.

Place the popping corn and oil in the centre of a double-thickness of aluminium foil. Bundle-wrap (see page 15) leaving plenty of room for the corn to pop around and expand. Place the package over a hot grill and shake occasionally using long-handled tongs. When the popping has ceased, pour the popcorn into a bowl and, if you wish, mix in some golden syrup.

Grilled stuffed mushrooms

Makes 24

24 large mushrooms

6 shallots, finely chopped

1 medium-size sweet red pepper, de-seeded and finely chopped

4 large garlic cloves, crushed

2 tablespoons finely chopped parsley

75g (2oz) fresh white breadcrumbs

50g (2oz) butter, melted

garlic salt and freshly ground black pepper

3$\frac{1}{2}$floz (100ml) virgin olive oil

2 tablespoons lemon juice

1 tablespoon lime juice or dry white wine

To make the marinade, mix the ingredients in a shallow dish and blend well.

Remove stems from the mushrooms and finely chop. Place the caps in the marinade, cover the bowl, and leave in a cool place for 2-3 hours. Turn the mushrooms occasionally. Drain the caps and preserve the remaining marinade.

Prepare the barbecue for grilling, following the instructions on page 8.

Heat the oil, either in a frying pan or on the barbecue's griddle plate, and sauté the shallots, red pepper, chopped mushroom stalks and garlic for about 5 minutes or until the shallots have softened. Add the parsley and mix all together with 4 tablespoons of the reserved marinade. Mix in the breadcrumbs and season to taste with the garlic salt and black pepper.

Brush the tops of the mushroom caps with melted butter and place upside down on the oiled grill or oiled griddle plate. Lightly fill the caps with the prepared stuffing and cook for about 10 minutes until well heated through.

Serve immediately.

Bruschetta

The perfect appetiser for a gathering of garlic devotees.

Serves 4

1 french bread-stick*

4 large garlic cloves (use 1 clove for every 2-3 slices of bread)

extra virgin olive oil

salt and freshly ground black pepper

Prepare the barbecue for grilling, following the instructions on page 8.

Cut the bread into thick slices and toast over high heat. Rub one side of the toasted bread with garlic. Drizzle plenty of olive oil over the bread and season to taste with salt and pepper.

* or use day-old Ciabatta or Foccacia.

19

appetisers

Prawns with a hint of mint and garlic

Served hot from the grill, these flavourful prawns make delicious appetisers

Serves 6-8

Makes about 60

1kg (2 lb) medium size prawns, peeled and de-veined

Marinade:

1 large or 2 medium garlic cloves, crushed

1½ tablespoons chopped fresh mint or 1 rounded teaspoon dried mint

1 teaspoon salt

¼ teaspoon freshly ground black pepper

1 teaspoon chilli powder

1 tablespoon red or white wine vinegar

1 teaspoon dried basil

150ml (¼ pint) oil

To make the marinade, mix together the ingredients in a bowl. Add the prawns and turn until well coated with the marinade. Cover and refrigerate for 5-7 hours or overnight.

Prepare the barbecue for grilling, following the instructions on page 8.

Briefly drain the prawns and reserve the marinade. Thread the prawns on to the skewers and place on the grill, or greased griddle plate. Cook over medium heat for 4-5 minutes, turning once and basting frequently with the marinade. Do not overcook.

Serve hot.

Scallop and mushroom Teriyaki

Makes 12

12 scallops out of their shells, washed and dried

4 tablespoons soy sauce

40g (1½oz) soft brown sugar

2 tablespoons groundnut oil or sunflower oil

1 tablespoon mirin or dry sherry

1 teaspoon freshly grated root ginger or a pinch of ground ginger

1 garlic clove, crushed

12 closed-cap mushrooms, stalks removed

Prepare the barbecue for grilling, following the instructions on page 8.

Place the scallops in a bowl. Mix together the soy sauce, sugar, oil, mirin or sherry, ginger and garlic. Pour the mixture over the scallops, stir gently to coat and leave them to marinate for about 10 minutes. Remove the scallops, reserving the marinade.

Place a scallop in each mushroom cup and thread them onto skewers, taking care that the scallops are held securely. Grill, over medium to high heat, for about 5 minutes or until the scallops are opaque and firm. Turn and baste frequently with the reserved marinade. Serve immediately.

Wing drumsticks Teriyaki

Makes 20

20 meaty chicken wings

Teriyaki:

1$\frac{1}{2}$ tablespoons clear honey

1$\frac{1}{2}$ tablespoons groundnut or sunflower oil

4 tablespoons soy sauce

1 tablespoon dry red wine or red wine vinegar

1 teaspoon freshly grated root ginger or $\frac{1}{2}$ teaspoon ground ginger

1 large garlic clove, crushed

Cut through the wing joints and set the joint, with the pointed tip, to one side for further use.

Using a small sharp knife, carefully loosen the flesh around the lower joints of the remaining wing portions and push down so that they resemble mini-lollipops. Place the prepared wing pieces in a bowl and pour over the marinade.

Cover the bowl with food wrap and leave for 2-3 hours in a cool place, or overnight in the refrigerator turning the drumsticks occasionally.

Prepare the barbecue for 'Indirect heat' cooking, following the instructions on page 10. Drain the chicken pieces and reserve the marinade. Cook the drumsticks on the barbecue at medium to high heat, with the lid down, for 20-30 minutes, or until cooked and sporting a dark golden/mahogany colour. (Basting frequently with the reserved marinade will result in the drumsticks taking on a dark mahogany hue.)

See also alternative cooking suggestion.

Chicken wings with honey glaze

(pictured on page 16)

Cooking wing pieces in this quantity is easier if you use a large, hinged wire broiler. Remember to oil the inside of the broiler before placing the chicken pieces in it.

Makes 40

20 meaty chicken wings

1 quantity of soy sake marinade (page 154)

Cut the wings through the joints and discard the bony tips. Place the chicken pieces in a large bowl and pour over the marinade. Cover and leave for 2-3 hours at room temperature or overnight in a refrigerator (turning the pieces occasionally, if possible).

Prepare the barbecue for grilling, following the instructions on page 8.

Drain the chicken pieces and reserve the marinade. Grill the pieces over medium to high heat for about 15 minutes or until cooked and a dark mahogany hue.

Baste the chicken pieces frequently during the final few minutes of cooking.

Alternative cooking suggestion:

Note: If you prefer to grill the wing drumsticks over direct heat, reduce the cooking time to about 15 minutes and baste the chicken occasionally with some of the reserved marinade.

21

appetisers

Spicy cheesy potato slices

(pictured on page 16)

One of the tastiest, and undoubtedly one of the cheapest, appetisers around.

Makes about 40

4 large baking potatoes

75g (3oz) butter, softened

1 tablespoon barbecue spice

$^1/_2$ teaspoon garlic salt

25g (1oz) grated parmesan cheese

Prepare the barbecue for grilling, following the instructions on page 8.

Cut the potatoes lengthways into slices about 5mm ($^1/_4$ inch) thick, discarding the outer slices. Dry the slices with kitchen paper.

Mix together the butter, barbecue spice and garlic salt.

Brush the slices generously with the spicy butter turn and cook on a griddle plate or grill, over high heat for 4-5 minutes. Baste the uncooked side with the butter and cook for a further 3-4 minutes or until the potato slices feel soft when pierced with a skewer. Sprinkle grated parmesan over the slices soon after turning.

To serve individual slices as an appetiser, pierce the edge of each slice with two wooden cocktail sticks, roughly 1cm ($^1/_2$ inch) apart. Bringing the ends of the sticks together will enable one to hold and eat the slice decorously.

Spicy grilled prawns

(pictured on page 16)

Makes about 60

1kg (2 lb) medium-sized prawns, peeled and de-veined

3$^1/_2$ tablespoons melted butter or margarine

Marinade:

1 teaspoon salt

$^1/_2$ teaspoon freshly ground black pepper

$^1/_2$ teaspoon garlic powder

4 tablespoons chilli sauce

4 tablespoons red or white wine vinegar

2 tablespoons Worcestershire sauce

4 tablespoons finely chopped fresh parsley

3 tablespoons oil

To make the marinade, mix the ingredients in a bowl and blend well. Add the prawns and turn until completely coated with the marinade. Cover the bowl and refrigerate for 1-3 hours.

Prepare the barbecue for grilling, following the instructions on page 8.

Drain the prawns and reserve the marinade. Blend the reserved marinade with the melted butter or margarine. Thread the prawns on to skewers and place them on the grill. Cook over a medium heat for 6-8 minutes, turning once and basting the prawns frequently and generously with the marinade mixture during cooking. Do not overcook the prawns as this will make them chewy.

Hot 'n' spicy bumper burger

A giant burger that will provide up to eight people with something to get their teeth into.

Serves 6-8

1 round bread cob about 25cm (10 inches) in diameter, or 2 pitta breads

1 quantity of garlic butter or tarragon and parsley butter (pages 160 and 161) at room temperature

1kg (2 lb) chuck steak, minced finely

1 large onion, chopped finely

$\frac{1}{2}$ teaspoon mustard powder

1 tablespoon soy sauce

1 tablespoon chilli sauce

2 teaspoons horseradish sauce

$\frac{1}{4}$ teaspoon ground ginger

1 tablespoon Worcestershire sauce

To Serve:

1 large red onion, sliced thinly (optional)

2 large tomatoes, sliced thinly

1 avocado, sliced thinly

shredded lettuce

Slice the cob in half horizontally. If pitta bread is used, part-slice these horizontally and lift open to make a large, hinged flat bread. Spread the cut surfaces of either bread with the flavoured butter.

In a large bowl mix together the meat, onion, mustard, soy sauce, chilli sauce, horseradish sauce, ginger and Worcestershire sauce. Shape the mixture into one large burger lightly bigger in diameter than the cob or opened out pitta bread.

Prepare the barbecue for grilling, following the instructions on page 8. Oil a large, hinged broiler and place the burger inside. Alternatively, place the burger directly on to a greased grill or a greased griddle plate. Cook the burger over high heat for 6-10 minutes per side or until cooked to the desired degree. If cooking directly on the grill, use 2 rimless baking sheets - one slipped under the burger and one on top - to turn the burger. Once turned, place the bread, cut side down, to toast on the grill.

To garnish and serve, place the burger on the bottom half of the cob, or on one side of the pitta breads and top with onion slices (if used), tomato slices, avocado slices, shredded lettuce and remaining bread. Cut into the required number of wedges and serve immediately.

Beefand**Veal**

Red wine burgers

Serves 6-8

50g (2oz) butter

2 medium-size onions, chopped finely

5 tablespoons dry red wine

750g (1¹/₂ lb) finely minced chuck steak

40g (1¹/₂oz) fresh breadcrumbs

1 teaspoon salt

¹/₄ teaspoon freshly ground black pepper

1 egg beaten

6-8 soft rolls

Prepare the barbecue for grilling, following the instructions on page 8. Place half the butter, onion and red wine vinegar on one side. Lightly mix the remaining wine, butter and onion into the meat. Stir in the breadcrumbs, salt, pepper and egg. Shape the mixture into 6-8 burgers approximately 2cm (³/₄ inch) thick.

Melt the reserved butter in a small saucepan, add the reserved onion and fry gently until transparent. Add the reserved wine and simmer for about 5 minutes. Brush the wine sauce over the burgers and grill, or cook on a greased griddle plate, over medium to high heat, for about 8-10 minutes each side. Brush the sauce over the burgers occasionally during cooking. Toast the rolls during the last few minutes of cooking. Fill the rolls with the burgers, garnish if wished and serve.

Teriyaki beef strips

Serves 6-8

1kg (2 lb) sirloin steak 2cm (³/₄ inch) thick, cut into 6mm (¹/₄ inch) thick slices

oil for greasing

Marinade:

6 tablespoons soy sauce or shoyu sauce

2 tablespoons dry red wine, red wine vinegar or sake

1 teaspoon ground ginger

1¹/₂ tablespoons oil

1 garlic clove, chopped very finely

1-3 teaspoons brown sugar, to taste

To make the marinade, mix together the ingredients in a bowl. Add the meat strips and turn until well coated with the marinade. Cover the bowl and place in the refrigerator for 3-4 hours.

Prepare the barbecue for grilling, following the instructions on page 8.

Lift the meat from the bowl, drain briefly and reserve the marinade.

Thread the meat, snake-fashion, onto 15-20cm (6-8 inches) long, oiled skewers. Grill the meat over medium to high heat for just 1-2 minutes on each side, basting once or twice with the marinade. Avoid over-cooking the meat and serve immediately.

Aloha burgers

Because of its 'arresting' nature (the spicy beef and juicy pineapple combine very nicely), I was tempted (almost) to dedicate this recipe to the constabulary and give it the title 'aloha – aloha'.

Serves 6

750g (1½ lb) lean minced beef

1 teaspoon salt

¼ teaspoon freshly ground black pepper

2 teaspoons soy sauce

6 slices of canned pineapple plus 2 tablespoons juice

50g (2oz) brown sugar

1 teaspoon Worcestershire sauce

6 tablespoons tomato ketchup

Note: **If using fresh pineapple, add 2 tablespoons of pineapple or orange juice.**

Prepare the barbecue for grilling, following the instructions on page 8.

Mix together the minced beef, salt, pepper and soy sauce in a large bowl. Shape the mixture into 6 burgers slightly larger in diameter than the pineapple slices. Press a pineapple slice into the surface of each burger and mould the meat around it to hold the slice firmly in place.

Place the pineapple juice, sugar, Worcestershire sauce and tomato ketchup in a small saucepan and heat gently for a few minutes. Brush the hot sauce over the pineapple surface of the burger. Grill, or cook on a greased griddle plate, over medium to high heat, for about 10 minutes, or until the meat is done. Brush the burgers frequently with the sauce during cooking to give a glaze to the pineapple slices.

BeefandVeal

Stuffed rump steak with tarragon & parsley butter

Serves 4

750g (1¹/₂ lb) rump steak, cut about
4cm (1¹/₂ inches) thick

1 quantity of tarragon and parsley
butter (page 161), chilled

oil for brushing

Stuffing:

1 teaspoon finely chopped shallot
or onion

a little oil

125g (4oz) open mushrooms,
chopped finely

1 teaspoon finely chopped fresh parsley

1 garlic clove, crushed

1 rounded tablespoon finely chopped
cooked ham

1 tablespoon fresh breadcrumbs

salt and freshly ground black pepper

To prepare the stuffing, in a pan cook the shallot or onion in a little oil until soft. Add the mushrooms, parsley and garlic, cover the pan and cook over medium heat for about 5 minutes. Add the ham, breadcrumbs and salt and pepper and stir lightly to mix. Turn the mixture on to a plate to cool.

Prepare the barbecue for grilling, following the instructions on page 8.

Slit the steak on side to form a deep pocket. Push the stuffing well into the pocket and close the opening with a trussing needle and string or a fine skewer. Slice the butter into pats. Brush the steak with oil and grill, over medium to high heat, for about 4-5 minutes on each side, or until cooked to the desired degree. Remove the string or skewer. Cut the steak into 1cm (¹/₂ inch) thick slices and serve with the flavoured butter.

Stir-fried steak in oyster sauce

Serves 4-6

750g (1 1/2 lb) rump or fillet beef steak, sliced thinly

1 tablespoon cornflour

1/2 teaspoon salt

4 tablespoon oil

1 tablespoon soy sauce

2 tablespoons oyster sauce

1/2 chicken stock cube, crushed

2 tablespoons dry sherry

freshly ground black pepper

Prepare the barbecue for wok-cooking, following the instructions on page 14.

Cut the steaks across the grain into 5cm (2 inch) strips the thickness of a pencil. Sprinkle with the cornflour and the salt, and pepper to taste, and mix together lightly

Heat the wok on the barbecue, add the oil and, when very hot, add the beef, spreading the strips evenly. Stir-fry over high heat for 1 minute. Add the soy and oyster sauces, the crushed stock cube and the sherry. Stir-fry for a further 1 minute and then turn out on to a warmed dish.

Serve immediately, with rice or noodles.

Steak au poivre flambé

This recipe provides the cook with a great opportunity to add a little extra drama and excitement to his, or her, barbecue performance.

Serves 4

2 tablespoons black peppercorns, crushed coarsely

4 fillet or rump steaks about 2.5cm (1 inch) thick

50g (2oz) butter

2 large tomatoes, sliced thickly

a pinch of fresh or dried oregano

a pinch of garlic salt

4 tablespoons brandy

Press the peppercorns firmly into both sides of the meat. Leave the steaks at room temperature for 30-40 minutes. Prepare the barbecue for grilling, following the instructions on page 8. Grill the meat over high heat until cooked to the desired degree (about 5 minutes per side for rare). When cooked, transfer the meat to a hot, shallow dish.

Melt the butter in a frying pan, add the tomato slices and heat through. Season with the oregano and garlic salt. Arrange the tomato slices on top of the steaks. Warm the brandy, spoon it evenly over the steaks and ignite. Serve it as soon as the flames subside.

Quick-fried beef with Chinese leaves

Quick, easy and tasty. All in all, quite a 'stirring' little recipe!

Serves 4

500g (1 lb) fillet or rump steak

750g (1¹/₂ lb) Chinese lettuce leaves

Marinade:

1 teaspoon sake or dry sherry

1 teaspoon soy sauce

¹/₂ teaspoon sugar

1 teaspoon sesame oil

1 yolk from a standard (size 3) egg

4 tablespoons vegetable oil

3 teaspoons cornflour

3 tablespoons oyster sauce

1 teaspoon sesame oil

¹/₂ teaspoon sugar

2 tablespoons cold water

salt and freshly ground black pepper

Prepare the barbecue for wok-cooking, following the instructions on page 14.

Combine all the marinade ingredients in a bowl.

Slice the beef into thin slices (part-freezing the meat beforehand will help) about 5-6cm (2-2¹/₂ inches) in length. Add to the bowl and leave to marinate in a cool place for about an hour.

Cut the Chinese leaves into 5cm (2 inch) lengths.

Position the wok on the barbecue and heat two tablespoons of oil therein. Add the Chinese leaves and stir fry until tender. Season the leaves and arrange over the bottom of a large platter. Drain the beef from the marinade, sprinkle over with the cornflour and mix together. Heat the remaining two tablespoons of oil in the wok and stir-fry the beef strips until golden brown. Remove the beef from the wok and keep warm. Add the oyster sauce to the wok, and when it begins to bubble, return the beef to the wok along with the sesame oil, sugar and water. Keep stirring until the sauce thickens and the beef is heated through.

Spread the beef evenly over the Chinese leaves and serve immediately.

Teriyaki flank steak

This recipe is best with thick flank, so request this specially from your butcher. Teriyaki flank steak sandwiches are hard to beat, be the meat hot or cold.

Serves 4-6

750g (1 1/2 lb) whole flank steak

Marinade:

6 tablespoons soy sauce

**150ml (1/4 pint) red wine
or red wine vinegar**

**2 teaspoons freshly grated root ginger
or 1/2 teaspoon ground ginger**

1 garlic clove, chopped very finely

**2 tablespoons brown sugar,
packed firmly**

2 tablespoons lemon juice

2 tablespoons oil

1 medium-size onion, chopped finely

1/4 teaspoon freshly ground black pepper

Give the steak a firm beating with a rolling pin or wooden steak hammer. Place the steak in a shallow dish. Mix together all the ingredients for the marinade and pour over the meat. Cover and leave in the refrigerator for at least 6 hours or overnight.

Prepare the barbecue for grilling, following the instructions on page 8.

Lift the steak from the marinade and drain briefly. Reserve the marinade. Place the steak on the grill, or greased griddle plate, and cook, over high heat, for about 5 minutes each side, basting occasionally with the marinade. (Flank should only be served rare for, despite marinating, 'medium to well-done' steaks usually turn out a little leathery.) To serve the steak, slice it thinly at an angle of 45 degrees.

BeefandVeal

Grilled meat tarts with mushroom and onion filling

(pictured on page 112)

Serves 6

750g (1 1/2 lb) lean beef, minced finely

3 tablespoons fine dry breadcrumbs

1 egg

2 tablespoons soft butter

1 tablespoon finely chopped onion

250g (8oz) closed-cap mushrooms, sliced

75g (3oz) grated cheddar cheese

salt and freshly ground pepper

Prepare the barbecue for grilling, following the instructions on page 8.

Place the minced beef, breadcrumbs, 1/2 teaspoon of salt, 1/4 teaspoon of pepper and egg in a bowl and blend carefully. Divide the mixture into 6 equal portions. Form each portion into a 1cm (1/2 inch) patty, about 10cm (4 inches) in diameter. *Lightly* press each patty into an aluminium foil individual tart mould, covering the bottom and sides.

Place the moulds upside down on the grill and cook, over medium heat, until the meat just starts to turn brown. Take care not to overcook the meat or it will become dry.

Whilst the meat is cooking, melt the butter in a small pan and cook the onion until just golden. Add the mushrooms, season to taste and cook until soft.

Fill the meat shells with the onion mixture and sprinkle over the grated cheese. Continue cooking the meat tarts until the cheese melts. Closing the barbecue lid helps melt the cheese. (The meat tarts can be cooked throughout by the 'Indirect heat' method if desired.)

Carefully remove the meat tarts from the foil moulds and serve immediately.

Steak with blue cheese butter

Serves 4-6

750g (1½ lb) whole flank steak

175ml (6floz) French dressing

1 tablespoon soft butter

75g (3oz) blue cheese

1 tablespoon chopped fresh rosemary or 1 teaspoon of dried rosemary

1 tablespoon finely chopped chives

1 garlic clove, chopped very finely

a pinch of dried oregano or dried basil

a pinch of freshly ground black pepper

Place the steak in a shallow dish and pour over the French dressing. Turn the steak 2 or 3 times; then cover the dish and place in the refrigerator for at least 4 hours or overnight. Blend together the butter, blue cheese, chives, garlic, rosemary and oregano or basil. Add a pinch of freshly ground black pepper. Chill if not using immediately.

Prepare the barbecue for grilling, following the instructions on page 8.

Lift the steak from the dish and drain briefly, Grill over high heat for 4-5 minutes per side - depending on the thickness of the steak. For best eating, the steak should be served rare (medium and well-done flank usually ends up being somewhat tough). Place the steak on a warm platter and slice thinly across the grain at an angle of 45 degrees.

Serve with a pat or spoonful of the blue cheese butter on each portion.

Roast beef of old England

(pictured opposite)

Some may disagree, but for me Roast beef, with its sidekick Yorkshire pudding, ranks alongside, and shares equal billing with, the quintessential 'Bread and Butter Pudding' (page 133).
Opening up the lid of your barbecue to reveal a delectable Fore rib in all its glory, is guaranteed to create havoc with bystanders' taste buds!
The visual impact will be compounded if a golden mound of Yorkshire pudding can be glimpsed beneath the grill bars.

Fore rib or Wing rib

(With bone in, allow about 375g (12oz) per serving, if joint is boned and rolled, allow about 250g (8oz) per serving.)

Trim excess fat from the meat, wipe the joint and rub salt and freshly ground black pepper into it. Securely tie the joint with twine at 2.5cm (1 inch) intervals.

Prepare the barbecue for 'Indirect heat' cooking, following the instructions on page 10.

Roast the meat, using a medium heat setting, until cooked to the desired degree. See the cooking time chart on page 184 for further information.

Should you wish to offer Yorkshire pudding to your family and guests, make up your usual pudding mix about an hour or so before the roast has finished cooking. Having allowed the pudding mixture to stand for about 30 minutes or so, gently pour it through the grill bars of the barbecue into the drip pan containing the hot fats and juices that have fallen from the joint above.

Continue cooking, with the lid of the barbecue in the closed position, for the last 30 minutes of cooking time or until the pudding has become puffed up and golden.

Allow the joint to rest for at least 10 minutes to allow its juices to settle.

Pictured opposite:
Roast beef of old England

Barbecued boeuf
en croûte

(pictured on page 36)

Boeuf en Croûte (Beef Wellington) is a spectacular dish to serve up at dinner parties and relatively easy to prepare. Although somewhat expensive when compared to other dishes, the cost per head compares very favourably to providing each guest with, say, a decent size Pizza. Apart from beef, barbecuing 'en croûte' can be applied to boned venison, lamb, chicken or large fish such as salmon and sea trout.

I recommend that the preparation, detailed on the next page, is carried out the day before the event. It can be carried out on the actual day, providing the part-cooked meat is quite cold, and the pastry well chilled, before preparing the dish.

Serves 6

1kg (2 lb) fillet of beef

brandy for brushing

75g (3oz) butter

1 Spanish onion, chopped finely

250g (8oz) closed-cap button mushrooms, chopped finely

2 teaspoons chopped mixed fresh herbs

500g (1 lb) packet of puff pastry, chilled well

1 egg, beaten well

a little red wine

salt and freshly ground pepper

fresh watercress or parsley to garnish

The day before, or early on the day itself, preheat the oven to Gas Mark 7/220°C/425°F.

Trim the excess fat from the fillet and tie it into a compact shape. Brush the fillet generously with brandy.

Melt 25g (1oz) of the butter in a roasting tin. Increase the heat, add the meat and brown it quickly all over. Then roast the meat in the oven for 15 minutes, basting it occasionally with the pan juices.

Remove the meat from the oven and allow it to get cold. Remove the string and place the meat in the refrigerator. Reserve the pan juices for making gravy.

The next day, melt the remaining butter in a small saucepan, add the onion and cook for about 5 minutes. Add the mushrooms and mixed herbs and continue cooking over a gentle heat until the mixture is fairly concentrated (this takes about 20 minutes). Season the mixture with salt and pepper and put on one side to cool.

Prepare the barbecue for 'Indirect heat' cooking, following the instructions on page 10.

Roll out the pastry to a rectangle about 38 x 25cm (15 x 10 inches). Reserve the edge trimmings for decoration.

Spread half the mushroom mixture over the centre of the pastry and place the meat on top. Spread the remaining mushroom mixture over the fillet. Brush the edge of the pastry with some of the beaten egg and wrap the pastry around the fillet, pressing the edges firmly together. Brush any excess pastry at the ends with more of the egg and double-fold. Cut out diamond shapes from the reserved pastry, moisten with more of the beaten egg and use to decorate the pastry. Brush the pastry all over with the rest of the egg.

Carefully place the pastry-wrapped beef on a baking sheet and bake, with medium to high heat, for 35-40 minutes, or until the pastry is well browned.

Add some red wine to the reserved pan juices and simmer to reduce slightly. Keep warm.

Cut the beef into thick slices and serve it, garnished with watercress or parsley, with the gravy.

Veal and streaky kebabs

Serves 4

500g (1 lb) lean shoulder of veal or veal fillet

6 rashers of streaky bacon

250g (8oz) button mushrooms

1 large green pepper, de-seeded, grilled and skinned, cut into 2.5cm (1 inch) squares

a pinch of ground ginger

a pinch of ground mace

a pinch of ground nutmeg

75g (3oz) butter

salt and freshly ground black pepper

Prepare the barbecue for grilling, following the instructions on page 8.

Cut the veal into 2-2.5cm (³/₄ inch -1 inch) cubes. Roll up each rasher of bacon and cut in half to make 2 rolls.

Thread the bacon, veal, mushrooms and green pepper on to metal skewers, making sure that a roll of bacon is nestling against each cube of veal. Sprinkle the meat with the spices and seasonings and dot with the butter.

Grill, over medium heat, for about 15-20 minutes, turning the kebabs frequently, or until the bacon and veal kebabs are cooked.

Skewered veal and ham olives

(pictured opposite)

This dish can also be made using escalopes of pork. I personally like the strong scent and flavour from the sage but, if preferred, use leaves of basil or mint.

Serves 4

4 veal escalopes, cut into thin 10-13cm (4-5 inch) squares

lemon juice to taste

4 thin slices of cooked ham, cut into 10-13cm (4-5 inches) squares

4 rashers of streaky bacon, sliced thinly

2 medium-size onions, cut into 5mm (¹/₄ inch) thick slices

sage leaves

2 tablespoons melted bacon fat or dripping

salt and freshly ground black pepper

Prepare the barbecue for grilling, following the instructions on page 8.

Season the escalopes with lemon juice and salt and pepper. Lay a slice of ham on each escalope. Roll up the meat and tightly wrap a piece of streaky bacon around each roll.

Thread two veal and ham olives on to a skewer or, preferably, two skewers spaced about 4cm (1¹/₂ inches) apart. Do the same with the other two olives. Alternate each olive with a slice of onion and a sage leaf.

Brush the olives with the melted bacon fat or dripping and grill, over medium heat, for about 8 minutes or until cooked through. Turn and baste a few times during cooking.

Pictured opposite:
Skewered veal and ham olives
Barbecued boeuf en croûte

BeefandVeal

Brandied sirloin, spit-roasted with a mustard coating

Serves 6-8

1.25-1.75kg (3-4 lb) sirloin of beef

Marinade:

4 tablespoons brandy

150ml ($^{1}/_{4}$ pint) apple juice

150ml ($^{1}/_{4}$ pint) sunflower oil

2 garlic cloves, chopped very finely

$^{1}/_{4}$ teaspoon pepper

Mustard coating:

2 tablespoons wholegrain mustard

$^{1}/_{2}$ teaspoon freshly ground black pepper

55ml (2floz) single cream

Combine the marinade ingredients and stir well. Place the meat in a baking dish and pour the marinade over. Cover the dish with food wrap and leave the meat, turning occasionally, to marinate in the refrigerator overnight, or for as long as possible during the day of cooking.

Prepare the gas barbecue for spit-roasting, following the instructions on page 12. Remove the meat from the marinade, drain briefly and pat all over with kitchen towel.

Insert the spit through the centre of the sirloin and test for balance (see page 12) before tightening the spit forks. If deemed necessary, tie the meat securely with string at regular intervals to retain the shape of the joint.

Prepare the mustard coating by combining the mustard, pepper and cream.

Spread the paste evenly over the surface of the meat. Position a drip pan to catch the juices falling from the meat as it rotates.

Cook the sirloin with the burners set to medium heat and the lid of the barbecue in the down position.

If the lid of the barbecue has to be open whilst cooking the meat, adjust the heat control to medium/high.

Cooking time will depend upon all the usual variables, ie. weight of the joint, desired degree of doneness, lid set in the open or closed position and the state of the weather, but for medium to rare meat reckon on 2-2$^{1}/_{2}$ hours. Otherwise test with a meat thermometer until the reading registers around 80°C (150°F).

If desired, skim the fats from the roasting juices and whisk together with some of the reserved marinade to serve separately as a sauce.

Beef and courgette kebabs

Serves 4

1kg (2 lb) rump, sirloin or fillet steak

2 courgettes

3 tablespoons groundnut oil

3 tablespoons soft butter

1 garlic clove, crushed

$^1/_4$ teaspoon freshly ground black pepper

4 medium-size tomatoes, quartered

Trim the meat and cut into 2.5cm (1 inch) cubes.

Slice the courgettes into circles about 1cm ($^1/_2$ inch) thick. Blanch them in a pan of boiling water for 30 seconds. Drain well.

Prepare the barbecue for grilling, following the instructions on page 8.

Place the oil, butter, garlic and pepper in a small saucepan and heat gently for a few minutes. Keep the pan on the side of the grill for basting.

Thread the meat cubes, courgette slices and tomato pieces alternately on to skewers and brush with the garlic oil.

Grill over medium to high heat, turning and basting frequently, for about 10 minutes or until cooked to the desired degree.

Rib eye steaks with rosemary

Serves 4

4 rib eye steaks cut 2-2.5cm ($^3/_4$-1 inch) thick

1 tablespoon oil

2 tablespoons chopped fresh rosemary or 2 teaspoons dried rosemary

salt and freshly ground pepper

Brush the steaks all over with the oil and press equal portions of the rosemary into both sides. Leave the steaks at room temperature for about 30 minutes.

Prepare the barbecue for grilling, following the instructions on page 8.

Grill the steaks, with medium heat, until cooked to the desired degree. Carefully turn the steaks over, half way through cooking. Season with salt and freshly ground pepper and serve with salad or vegetables in season.

To provide each of your guests with a steak, cooked to suit their individual requirements, try cutting the steaks to different thicknesses before proceeding to cook them in concert, ie. if the steaks are placed on the grill together and come off the grill at the same time, having followed the above recipe and the chart on page 185 as a guide, you should - all being well - end up by serving rare, medium or well done steaks to order. The 'well-doners' might however object to the 'under-doners' getting a bigger slice of the cake!

BeefandVeal

Roast veal

Serve this with veal forcemeat or stuffing balls, and cook them alongside the roast during the last 40 minutes or so of cooking.

Serves 6

1.75kg (4 lb) loin, leg or shoulder of veal, boned and rolled

flour for sprinkling

8 rashers of streaky bacon

50g (2oz) fat, preferably dripping

salt and freshly ground pepper

Stand the joint in a roasting tin, sprinkle with flour and season lightly. Lay the rashers of bacon evenly over the joint and spread the fat liberally over the whole joint.

Prepare the barbecue for 'Indirect heat' cooking, following the instructions on page 10.

Roast the joint, with medium to high heat, for about 20 minutes; then lower the heat to medium ,if using a gas barbecue, or remove some of the charcoal fire-bed, for the remaining cooking period. A 1.75kg (4 lb) veal joint should take $1^3/_4$-2 hours to cook until well-done. Allow the joint to rest for about 10 minutes before carving.

Stuffed veal chops

Serves 4

4 veal chops about 2.5cm (1 inch) thick

4 very thin slices of bacon

4 slices of Gruyere or Fontina cheese

1 tablespoon chopped fresh thyme or rosemary

oil for brushing

salt, freshly ground pepper and grated nutmeg

Prepare the barbecue for grilling, following the instructions on page 8.

Cut a deep pocket, almost to the bone, through the thick part of each chop. Slide a slice of bacon and a slice of cheese into each pocket, together with a sprinkling of the chopped herbs.

Lay the chops on a board and beat the open edges hard with a rolling pin or meat hammer.

Brush the chops with oil and season with salt, pepper and grated nutmeg.

Grill the chops, over medium heat, for about 8 minutes each side or until the cheese begins to melt and run out of the chops.

Serve immediately.

Lamb

Lambapple burgers

Serves 6

500g (1 lb) minced lamb

2 tablespoons chopped fresh parsley

a generous pinch of dried rosemary

2 teaspoons soy sauce

$^1/_4$ teaspoon salt

a pinch of freshly ground pepper

275g (9oz) can of pineapple slices

50g (2oz) soft brown sugar

2 teaspoons Worcestershire sauce

6 tablespoons tomato ketchup

Prepare the barbecue for grilling, following the instructions on page 8.

Place the minced lamb, herbs, soy sauce and salt and pepper in a bowl and mix together. Lightly press the mixture into 6 burger shapes. Drain the pineapple slices and reserve about 2 tablespoons of the juice.

Press a pineapple slice into the surface of each burger and mould the minced meat up and around the edge of the pineapple slice.

Place the sugar, Worcestershire sauce, tomato sauce and reserved pineapple juice in a pan and heat gently for a few minutes, stirring occasionally.

Brush the warmed sauce over the burgers and grill, or cook on a greased griddle plate, over medium to high heat, for about 10 minutes or until the meat is cooked. Baste frequently with the sauce to glaze the pineapple slices and close the barbecue lid for the final two minutes or so of cooking to enhance the glaze.

Andalusian lamb chops

Serves 6

6 lamb chump chops

Marinade:

2 tablespoons finely chopped onion

150ml ($^1/_4$ pint) dry sherry

1 bay leaf

$^1/_2$ teaspoon dried oregano

1 teaspoon dried basil

3 tablespoons tarragon vinegar

6 tablespoons oil

$^1/_2$ teaspoon freshly ground black pepper

Place the chops in a shallow dish. Mix together the marinade ingredients and pour over the meat. Cover and marinate overnight in the refrigerator, or for 4-6 hours at room temperature, turning the chops occasionally. If refrigerated, allow the meat to stand at room temperature for about an hour before cooking.

Prepare the barbecue for grilling, following the instructions on page 8.

Lightly drain the chops and reserve the marinade. Place the chops on the grill and cook, over medium to high heat, for about 10-12 minutes each side or until done to the desired degree, basting occasionally with the marinade.

Lamb

Spit-roasted leg of lamb with anchovies, garlic and rosemary

Serves 8-10

2.25-2.75kg (5-6 lb) leg of lamb

4 garlic cloves, peeled and sliced lengthwise into 3

2 x 50g (2oz) tins of anchovies - drained of oil

a few sprigs of rosemary

75g (3oz) unsalted butter, softened

juice of 1 lemon

freshly ground black pepper

Using a narrow bladed sharp knife, make 12 deep incisions into the fleshy side of the joint. Insert into these a garlic slice, half an anchovy and a small sprig of rosemary making sure they are well pushed in. Cream the remaining anchovies, butter and lemon juice together and spread the mixture over the joint. Grind black pepper over the buttered joint. Preheat and prepare the barbecue for spit roasting, following the instructions on page 12.

Insert the spit almost parallel to the bone and test for balance (see page 12) before tightening the spit forks. Cook the joint over medium heat, basting the meat once or twice with some of the juices from the drip pan. If you prefer your meat done a *la Francaise* (slightly pink in the centre) cook it for about 1¼ -1½ hours or until the temperature reading on a meat thermometer is 60-65°C/ 140-150°F.

Remove the joint from the spit, cover with foil and leave to rest for 15-20 minutes before carving.

Angela's heavenly minty lamb kebabs

Serves 4

750g (1½ lb) lean boneless lamb, cut into 2.5cm (1 inch) cubes

Marinade:

150g (5oz) carton natural yoghurt

1 tablespoon olive oil

1 teaspoon concentrated mint sauce

½ teaspoon freshly grated root ginger or ¼ teaspoon ground ginger

salt and freshly ground black pepper

Mix together the yoghurt, olive oil, mint sauce and ginger in a large bowl. Add the lamb and leave in a cool place to marinate for at least 3-4 hours.

Prepare the barbecue for grilling, following the instructions on page 8.

Drain the lamb, reserving the marinade, and thread onto oiled metal skewers, leaving a small gap between each cube.

Place the kebabs on the grill, or greased griddle plate, and cook, over medium heat, for about 10-15 minutes depending upon how well done you like your lamb. Turn the kebabs several times during cooking, basting occasionally with the reserved marinade.

Try serving with 'Brown rice and vegetable salad' (page 146).

Lamb satay

Serves 6

1kg (2 lb) fillet end leg of lamb

Marinade:

4 tablespoons soy sauce

3 garlic cloves, crushed

1 small onion, chopped finely

1 tablespoon lemon juice

1 tablespoon soft brown sugar

Satay sauce:

2 teaspoons oil

1 large garlic clove, crushed

3 tablespoons smooth peanut butter

1$\frac{1}{2}$ tablespoons soy sauce

2 teaspoons lemon juice

1 green or red chilli, chopped finely

50g (2oz) creamed coconut

3 tablespoons chicken stock

Cut the lamb into 2.5cm (1 inch) cubes, removing any fat or gristle. Mix together the ingredients for the marinade in a large bowl. Add the cubes of meat and turn to coat evenly with the marinade. Cover the bowl and leave, at room temperature, for about an hour.

Prepare the barbecue for grilling, following the instructions on page 8.

Meanwhile, prepare the sauce. Heat the oil in a saucepan and cook the garlic over low heat for 1-2 minutes. Add the peanut butter and cook, stirring, until it starts to darken. Add the soy sauce, lemon juice, chilli, creamed coconut and stock and bring slowly to the boil, stirring constantly. Remove the pan to a corner of the grill, or on the warming grill, and allow to simmer for 5-6 minutes, stirring occasionally. Keep the sauce warm.

Lightly drain the lamb cubes, discarding the marinade, and thread on to skewers, allowing a small gap between the cubes. Cook, over high heat, for 10-15 minutes until all the sides are browned.

Pour the prepared sauce into small individual warmed dishes and, with the meat, serve immediately.

Lamb

Cinnamon lamb cutlets

Serves 6

12 best end lamb cutlets

Marinade:

1½ teaspoons ground cinnamon

1 tablespoon brown sugar

3 tablespoons oil

6 tablespoons orange juice

¼ teaspoon freshly ground black pepper

¼ teaspoon salt

Place the cutlets in a shallow dish. Mix together the marinade ingredients. Pour the marinade over the meat, turning it once or twice so the cutlets are well coated. Cover and marinate at room temperature for about 4 hours, or overnight in a refrigerator, turning the cutlets twice during this period.

Prepare the barbecue for grilling, following the instructions on page 8.

Briefly drain the cutlets and reserve the marinade. Place the cutlets on the grill and cook, over medium heat, for about 25 minutes, turning and basting occasionally with the reserved marinade. Do not overcook.

Soy and ginger flavoured lamb cutlets

Teriyaki sauce is widely available from stores and supermarkets, or you can make your own following the recipe on page 155 (in which case you will have to omit the honey). The marinade in this recipe can also be used for chicken and pork.

Serves 6

12 best end lamb cutlets

Marinade:

3 tablespoons oil

1½ tablespoons Teriyaki sauce

1 tablespoon sake or white wine vinegar

1 tablespoon Dijon whole-grain mustard

1 small piece of fresh root ginger, peeled and grated

Place the cutlets in a shallow dish. Mix together the marinade ingredients and pour over the meat. Turn the meat once or twice so that it is evenly coated. Marinate at room temperature for about 2 hours, turning the cutlets twice.

Prepare the barbecue for grilling, following the instructions on page 8.

Briefly drain the cutlets and reserve the marinade. Place on the grill and cook, over medium heat, for about 15 minutes, turning and basting occasionally with the reserved marinade.

Lemony lamb leg steaks

Serves 4

**4 x 2-2.5cm (³/₄-1 inch)
thick lamb leg steaks**

Marinade:

150ml (¹/₄ pint) oil

6 tablespoons lemon juice

1 teaspoon salt

1 teaspoon dried oregano

1 medium-size onion, chopped finely

1 garlic clove, crushed

¹/₄ teaspoon freshly ground black pepper

Garnish:

fresh parsley and lemon slices

Place the leg steaks in a shallow dish. Mix together the ingredients for the marinade and pour it over the meat. Turn the meat twice to coat well. Cover the dish and leave for at least 4 hours at room temperature, or overnight in the refrigerator. If refrigerated, allow the meat to stand at room temperature for 2-3 hours before cooking.

Prepare the barbecue for grilling, following the instructions on page 8.

Remove the legs steaks from the marinade and drain briefly. Place the steaks on the grill, over medium to high heat, and cook for 6-7 minutes on each side, or until done to your liking. Garnish the steaks with parsley and lemon slices.

Harry's herb and honey roast lamb

Master Harry Cross, to whom this recipe is dedicated, is still a little lamb in the eyes of his nearest and dearest but I have a sneaking suspicion that he will turn out to be a veritable tiger on the rugby field (and elsewhere) in years to come.

Serves 6-8

2 best ends of neck lamb, chined

3 tablespoons clear honey, warmed

2 tablespoons chopped fresh mixed herbs (choose from mint, rosemary, thyme, marjoram or tarragon) or 3 teaspoons dried herbs

5 tablespoons fresh breadcrumbs

2 teaspoons grated lemon zest

salt and freshly ground black pepper

With a sharp, short-bladed knife carefully trim the meat and fat 2.5cm (1 inch) from the end of the rib bones on each joint.

Prepare the barbecue for 'Indirect heat' cooking, following the instructions on page 10.

Brush the surface of the lamb with the warm honey. Mix together the herbs, breadcrumbs, lemon zest, salt and pepper. Sprinkle the mixture evenly over the surface of fat.

Cook, with medium heat, for about 1¹/₄ hours or until cooked to the desired degree.
To serve, carve between the rib bones to yield 7-8 slices per best end of neck.

Lamb

Mint jelly glazed breast of lamb

A cheap, but nonetheless very tasty cut, that barbecues well. Apart from the bones, remember to remove the tough membrane.

Serves 4

1 large boned breast of lamb weighing about 750g (1½ lb)

75g (3oz) fresh white breadcrumbs

½ teaspoon concentrated mint sauce

grated zest and juice of 1 lemon

1 egg, beaten

mint jelly for glazing

salt and freshly ground black pepper

chopped fresh parsley to garnish

Prepare the barbecue for 'Indirect heat' cooking, following the instructions on page 10.

Season the boned breast of lamb with salt and pepper.

Mix together the breadcrumbs, mint sauce, lemon zest and juice and enough of the beaten egg to make a fairly stiff mixture.

Spread the mixture evenly over the cut side of the meat. Roll up the breast tightly and secure with strong string every 2.5cm (1 inch) along the roll.

Place on the grill and cook, over medium heat, for about 1¼ hours or until done to your liking. Spread a thin layer of mint jelly over the surface of the roll during the last 5-10 minutes of cooking time. Allow the meat to stand for about 10 minutes. To serve, carve the meat into thick slices and garnish with chopped parsley.

Sweet and sour shoulder of lamb

Serves 6

2 tablespoons red wine vinegar

1 tablespoon soy sauce

2 tablespoons apple or orange juice

1 tablespoon tomato purée

1 tablespoon mirin or dry sherry

1 garlic clove, chopped very finely

a pinch of ground ginger

1.75-2.25kg (4-5 lb) shoulder of lamb

salt and freshly ground black pepper

Combine the vinegar, soy sauce, fruit juice, tomato purée, mirin or sherry, garlic and ground ginger and put to one side.

Prepare the barbecue for 'Indirect heat' cooking, following the instructions on page 10.

Season the shoulder with salt and pepper. Place the shoulder, fat side up, on the grill. Cook, with medium heat, for about 1½ hours. (The exact time will depend on the shoulder weight and the required degree of cooking.) 30 minutes before the end of cooking, brush the shoulder generously with the prepared sweet and sour glaze.

Allow the roast to rest for about 15 minutes before carving.

Butterflied leg of lamb in a herb crust

(pictured page 49)

Apart from having to remove the bone (your butcher will do this for you if you ask him nicely) and having to stand duty whilst the meat is cooking, this is a great way to tackle a leg of lamb on your barbecue.

Serves 6-8

2.25-2.75kg (5-6 lb) leg of lamb

1 tablespoon chopped fresh rosemary or 1 teaspoon dried rosemary

1 tablespoon chopped fresh parsley or 1 teaspoon dried parsley

1 tablespoon very finely chopped dried onion

1 tablespoon dried whole marjoram

1 large bay leaf, crumbled finely

$1/4$ teaspoon ground ginger

1 teaspoon salt

2 tablespoons red or white wine vinegar

50g (2oz) brown sugar

150ml ($1/4$ pint) dry white or red wine

150ml ($1/4$ pint) stock made from chicken stock cubes

To butterfly the leg of lamb, cut down the length of the inside of leg, carefully trim the flesh from the bone and remove the bone. Then open out the leg meat and, if necessary, slash the thicker areas to help the meat lie flat.

Combine all the remaining ingredients in a pan and heat gently for 20 minutes, stirring the sauce occasionally. Brush the sauce all over the meat.

Prepare the barbecue for grilling, following the instructions on page 8.

Place the meat on the grill, with the uncut surface (the fat side) uppermost. Cook, over medium heat, for about 40-50 minutes, or until cooked to your taste, basting it frequently with the sauce and turning it occasionally. When cooked the lamb should have a scrumptious, somewhat crusty looking surface. To serve, slice the lamb thinly across the grain.

Crown of roast lamb

(pictured on opposite page)

A culinary work of art and a truly regal dish fit to grace any table. A crown roast may be embellished with cutlet frills and/or glace cherries but it looks quite beautiful unadorned. It is wise to order a crown from your butcher well in advance, but it is not all that difficult, albeit a little time consuming, to make up your own from two matching best ends as described below.

Serves 6

2 best ends of neck of lamb salt and freshly ground black pepper

Stuffing:

25g (1oz) butter

1 small onion, chopped finely

1 large cooking apple, peeled, cored and chopped finely

250g (8oz) pork sausage meat

3 tablespoons fresh breadcrumbs, toasted lightly

1 tablespoon finely chopped fresh parsley

40g (1½oz) walnuts, chopped finely

½ teaspoon dried thyme

With a sharp, short-bladed knife, trim the meat and fat 4cm (1½ inches) from the end of the rib bones on each joint and season. Using a trussing needle and fine string, sew the ends of the joints together back to back so the fat is inside and the bones curve upwards and outwards.

To make the stuffing, melt the butter in a pan and cook the onion gently until soft. Add the apple and continue cooking for a few minutes. Add the sausage meat and combine well with the onion and apple. Cook for a further 3-4 minutes. Stir in the breadcrumbs, parsley, walnuts and thyme.

Prepare the barbecue for 'Indirect heat' cooking, following the instructions on page 10.

Place the crown roast on a piece of aluminium foil slightly wider than the base of the roast. Spoon the stuffing into the cavity up to 2.5cm (1 inch) or so below the base of the trimmed bones (to allow space for the stuffing to rise). Cover the tips of the rib bones with foil to prevent charring.

Cook the lamb on the foil with medium heat, allowing 35 minutes per 500g (1 lb). For an un-stuffed crown roast, allow 30 minutes per 500g (1 lb).

To serve, stand the crown on a serving dish and remove the foil from each bone tip, replacing, if you wish, with a cutlet frill.

Allow two cutlets for each person.

Pictured opposite:
Butterflied leg of lamb in a herb crust
Crown of roast lamb
Spit-roasted leg of lamb with anchovies, garlic and rosemary

Lamb

Lamb noisettes with cheese

Serves 6

6 best end lamb noisettes, cut 2.5cm (1 inch) thick

175g (6oz) blue cheese or 75g (3oz) parmesan cheese, grated

50g (2oz) butter, softened

salt and freshly ground black pepper

Prepare the barbecue for grilling, following the instructions on page 8.

Season the noisettes with salt and pepper. Grill on one side, over medium heat, for about 8 minutes.

Blend the cheese and butter together with the salt and pepper and place on one side. Grill the other side of the noisettes for about 5 minutes and spread with cheese mixture. Grill the meat for a further 2-3 minutes. Serve immediately.

Turkistan kebabs

Centuries ago, the fierce Turkish warriors used their swords to impale pieces of meat for grilling over the camp fire. Thus, so it is believed, began the art of skewer cooking.

Serves 6

1kg (2 lb) lean boneless lamb

175g (6oz) suet

125g (4oz) onion, chopped finely

25g (1oz) fresh parsley, chopped finely

1 garlic clove, chopped very finely

1 teaspoon paprika

$^{1}/_{2}$ teaspoon freshly ground black pepper

2 teaspoon salt

2 teaspoon lemon juice

2 eggs

oil for brushing and greasing

Pass the meat and suet through the medium size disc of a grinder. Combine the meat/suet mixture with the onion, parsley, garlic, paprika, pepper, salt and lemon juice and pass through the grinder - this time fitted with the fine disc - again. Blend thoroughly. Add the eggs and, with wet hands, mix well. Chill the mixture in the refrigerator for about 30 minutes or until firm.

Prepare the barbecue for grilling, following the instructions on page 8.

Re-wet the hands and mould the meat mixture on to oiled skewers to form torpedo-shaped pieces about 7.5cm (3 inches) long and 2.5cm (1 inch) in diameter.

Brush the meat with oil and grill, over high heat, for 8-10 minutes, turning to brown all sides.

Lambs kidney brochettes with sauce Bercy

To add a little *je ne sais quoi* to this recipe, or indeed any other skewered lamb meat or offal dish, replace the metal skewers with sharpened branches from a mature rosemary bush. Leaving some leaves at the unsharpened end will not only help to provide a pleasant aroma during cooking, but will also prettify an otherwise plain offering.

Serves 4

12 lambs kidneys

3 tablespoons melted butter

Sauce Bercy:

75g (3oz) butter

1 tablespoon very finely chopped shallots

300ml ($^1/_2$ pint) dry white wine

2 teaspoons plain flour

1 tablespoon very finely chopped fresh parsley

salt and freshly ground black pepper

Remove the fat and fine skin from the kidneys. Split each one from the inside edge to within 1cm ($^1/_2$ inch) of the outer surface. Remove the white core from the inside. Thread the opened-out kidneys on to fine skewers using a wide 'stitch' across the back to hold them open.

Prepare the barbecue for grilling, following the instructions on page 8.

Prepare the sauce. Melt 25g (1oz) of the butter in a saucepan, add the shallots and cook until soft. Add the wine and simmer until the liquid has reduced by half. Mix the remaining butter and the flour to a paste and add a little at a time to the wine mixture. Cook, stirring, until the mixture thickens. Stir in the parsley and add salt and pepper to taste. Keep warm while cooking the kidneys.

Brush the kidneys with half the melted butter and grill, over medium to high heat, for about 3 minutes each side, basting occasionally with the remaining butter. Do not overcook them as kidneys can rapidly become tough.

Serve the kidneys with the sauce.

Lamb

Herb-stuffed lambs kidneys

Serves 4

12 lambs kidneys

12 rashers of prime streaky bacon

40g (1½oz) butter, melted

Herb stuffing:

75g (3oz) fresh white breadcrumbs

3 tablespoons chopped fresh mixed herbs (including parsley)

25g (1oz) butter

1 medium-size onion, chopped

1 large egg, beaten

salt and freshly ground black pepper

Garnish:
fresh watercress

Skin the kidneys. Partially slit each one lengthways and remove the core. Remove the rind from the bacon rashers and spread them out on the work surface.

To make the stuffing, mix the breadcrumbs and herbs together. Melt the butter in a pan and cook the onion until soft. Stir the onion mixture into the bread-crumbs and add enough beaten egg to bind the mixture. Season well with salt and pepper.

Prepare the barbecue for grilling, following the instructions on page 8.

Spoon the prepared stuffing into the kidneys, place them at one end of the bacon rashers and roll up to enclose the kidneys.

Thread the wrapped kidneys on to skewers and brush well with the melted butter. Grill, over medium to high heat, for about 4-5 minutes each side, or until the bacon starts to crisp. Do not overcook otherwise the kidneys will become tough and chewy.

Serve immediately, garnished with watercress.

Caul-wrapped marinated lamb's liver

Caul, a lace-like membrane of pork or lamb's fat, can be obtained from most traditional butchers. For culinary purposes it is used to provide some protection, to offal in particular, from oven or grill heat whilst, at the same time, acting as a natural fat baster. Some butchers will require notice of your requirement a day or two beforehand.

Serves 4-6

Fresh or dry-salted caul, preferably pork

500-750g (1-1$\frac{1}{2}$ lb) lamb's liver, in one piece

Marinade:

2 teaspoons paprika

$\frac{1}{2}$ teaspoon cumin

a pinch of cayenne pepper

1 teaspoon salt

2 teaspoons lemon juice

3 tablespoons olive oil

To serve:
red wine vinegar

freshly ground black pepper

If the caul is dry-salted, soak it in cold water for about 20 minutes to soften it. Remove it from the water and pat dry before use.

Combine the marinade ingredients in a large bowl and mix well.

Peel away the outer membrane from the liver and cut away any coarse tubes or fibrous connective tissue. Add the liver to the marinade and leave for about 30 minutes in a cool place.

Prepare the barbecue for grilling, following the instructions on page 8.

Remove the liver and reserve the marinade. Drain the liver and wrap it in the sheet of caul until it is completely enclosed. Cook the wrapped liver, with medium heat, for about 10 minutes on each side until nicely browned. Baste occasionally with the reserved marinade during cooking. The liver should be cooked when it feels firm when pressed lightly.

Leave the liver to rest in a warm place for about 10 minutes before carving into thick slices (the heart of the liver should be pink and juicy). Provide your guests with some red wine vinegar and freshly ground black pepper for sprinkling over the liver.

Best served with a salad.

Lamb

Orange, mint and ginger double lamb loin chops

The orange, mint and ginger marinade gives the lamb a fresh, slightly sharp, flavour.

Serves 4

4 x 2-2.5cm (³/₄-1 inch) thick lamb double loin chops

Marinade:
grated zest and juice of 1 large orange

3 tablespoons chopped fresh mint

1 teaspoon freshly grated root-ginger or ¹/₂ teaspoon ground ginger

Garnish:
fresh parsley and orange slices

Place the double loin chops in a shallow dish large enough for them to be accommodated side by side.

Mix together the ingredients for the marinade and pour over the meat. Turn the chops twice to coat well. Cover the dish with food wrap and leave for at least 3 hours at room temperature. If refrigerated, allow the meat to stand at room temperature for 2-3 hours before cooking.

Prepare the barbecue for grilling, following the instructions on page 8.

Remove the chops from the marinade and drain briefly. Place the chops on the grill, over medium to high heat, and cook for 6-7 minutes on each side, or until done to your liking.

Garnish the chops with parsley and half slices of orange.

Greek lamb kebabs

Serves 4

750g (1¹/₂ lb) lamb leg steaks

salt and freshly ground black pepper

1 teaspoon dried marjoram or 1 tablespoon chopped fresh marjoram

2 small onions, peeled and quartered

4 tablespoons olive oil

1 tablespoon lemon juice

8 bay leaves

Trim the lamb, and cut into 2cm (³/₄ inch) cubes. Place the meat cubes in a dish and season with the salt, pepper and marjoram. Break the onion into layers and add the thick outer layers to the dish. Add the oil and lemon juice, stir well and cover the dish with food wrap. Leave in a cook place to marinate for 3-4 hours.

Prepare the barbecue for grilling, following the instructions on page 8.

Divide the cubes of lamb between four skewers, impaling a piece of onion and half a bay leaf between every two pieces of meat.

Place the kebabs on the grill and cook, over medium heat, for about 10-15 minutes depending upon how well done you like your lamb. Turn the kebabs several times during cooking.

Try serving the kebabs on a bed of tomato salad with a garnish of lemon wedges.

Pork

Pork and apple burgers

The flavours of pork and apple combine well to make this one of my favourite burgers.

Serves 6

1kg (2 lb) minced lean pork

1 medium-sized apple, chopped finely

1 egg, beaten

75g (3oz) fresh breadcrumbs

1 teaspoon garlic salt

$1/4$ teaspoon onion salt

$1/4$ teaspoon freshly ground black pepper

2 tablespoons oil

6 hamburger rolls, halved

Prepare the barbecue for grilling, following the instructions on page 8.

Mix together the pork, apple, egg and enough of the breadcrumbs to give a firm, not too wet, mixture. Carefully shape into 6 burgers.

Blend together the garlic salt, onion, salt, pepper and oil and brush some of the mixture on one side of the burgers.

Grill the oiled surfaces of the burgers, or cook on a greased griddle plate, over medium to high heat, for about 10 minutes. Brush the burgers with the rest of the oil mixture, turn and cook the other sides for a further 10 minutes or until nicely browned.

Toast the rolls during the last few minutes of cooking. Serve the burgers in the prepared rolls with your favourite barbecue sauce. One of the recipes on page 157 might be to your taste.

Pork and apricot kebabs

Serves 4

500g (1 lb) pork tenderloin or boneless pork loin

8 shallots or 2 medium-sized onions

250g (8oz) can of apricot halves

175g (6oz) soft brown sugar

4 tablespoons apricot jam

6 tablespoons red or white wine vinegar

3 tablespoons soy sauce

1 teaspoon mustard powder

salt and freshly ground black pepper

Prepare the barbecue for grilling, following the instructions on page 8.

Cut the pork into 2.5cm (1 inch) cubes.

If using shallots, parboil them for about 5 minutes; if using onions, parboil them whole for about 6-7 minutes and then cut into quarters. Drain the apricot halves, reserving the juice.

Thread the pork cubes, shallots or onion quarters and apricot halves on to skewers.

Combine the remaining ingredients in a small saucepan and heat gently until the sugar has dissolved. Brush the kebabs all over with the mixture. Place them on the grill and cook, over medium heat, for about 15 minutes. Turn and baste the kebabs several times during cooking.

Note: pineapple chunks may be used instead of the apricot halves. In which case, replace the apricot jam with marmalade and half the wine vinegar with the same quantity of pineapple juice.

Pork

Sweet and sour pork

Serves 4

250g (8oz) lean pork

1 teaspoon soy sauce

1 teaspoon rice wine or dry sherry

1 teaspoon finely grated fresh root ginger

2 dried mushrooms or 2 open-cap mushrooms

medium-sized onion

1 medium-sized green pepper

25g (1oz) canned bamboo shoots

50g (2oz) carrot

900ml (1½ pints) oil for deep frying

1½ tablespoons cornflour

2 tablespoons vegetable oil

1 garlic clove, chopped finely

salt

Sauce:

6 tablespoons chicken stock

1½ tablespoons soy sauce

5 tablespoons sugar

1 tablespoon tomato ketchup

½ teaspoon salt

1 tablespoon cornflour, dissolved in 2 tablespoons water

4 tablespoons red or white wine vinegar

2 slices canned or fresh pineapple, cut into 6 pieces

Cut the pork into bite-sized cubes and combine with the soy sauce, rice wine or sherry and grated ginger. Leave to marinate for about 15 minutes.

If using dried mushrooms, soak them in warm water until soft; then remove. Discard the stalks of the dried or fresh mushrooms and cut the caps into thin slices.

Prepare the barbecue for wok-cooking, following the instructions on page 14.

Slice the onion into bite-size pieces. De-seed the pepper and cut it into bite-size pieces. Cut the bamboo shoots into thin slices. Slice the carrot into thin rounds and parboil in lightly salted water. Rinse with cold water and drain.

Add the oil for deep-frying to the wok. Position the wok on the barbecue and heat the oil, over high heat, to 180°C/350°F. Add the cornflour to the pork cubes and turn them until evenly coated. Deep-fry the cubes until they are golden brown; then remove from the wok and drain.

Pour off the oil from the wok and replace with the vegetable oil. Heat the oil and quickly stir-fry the garlic. Add the carrot, pepper, onion, mushrooms and bamboo shoots, stir-frying very briefly between each addition.

Mix together the chicken stock, soy sauce, sugar, ketchup and salt and add this to the vegetables. Bring the sauce rapidly to the boil and then quickly mix in the dissolved cornflour, stirring constantly. When the sauce has thickened, add the pork cubes and vinegar; then add the pineapple pieces and stir well.

Serve immediately.

Stir-fried pork with mushrooms and cabbage

Stir-frying can be likened to a dance - slow, quick, quick, slow. The first step in the dance is the patient preparation that needs to be carried out before heating the wok. Stir-frying the prepared food constitutes the quick-steps. This high speed action demands that the prepared food, cooking implements and serving dishes are easily to hand. The final slow step is when you sit down to savour and enjoy the food.

Serves 4

750g (1¹/₂ lb) lean pork, sliced thinly

1 teaspoon salt

1 tablespoon cornflour

3 tablespoons vegetable oil

500g (1 lb) spring cabbage

3 tablespoons lard

250g (8oz) open-cap mushrooms halved, or sliced, and stalks discarded

1¹/₂ tablespoons soy sauce

3 tablespoons chicken stock

¹/₂ teaspoon sesame oil

2 teaspoons sugar

Prepare the barbecue for wok-cooking, following the instructions on page 14.

Cut the pork into thin bite-size slices. Sprinkle with the salt, cornflour and 1 tablespoon of the vegetable oil and mix together lightly. Remove the tougher stems from the cabbage and cut the leaves into 5cm (2 inch) pieces.

Position the wok on the barbecue and melt the lard. When hot, add the mushrooms and cabbage. Stir-fry over high heat for 1¹/₂ minutes. Add the soy sauce and chicken stock and continue to stir-fry for 1 minute. Cover the wok and cook, over medium heat, for a further 2 minutes. Turn out the vegetables on to a warmed dish and cover. Pour the remaining vegetable oil into the wok and, when hot, add the pork and stir-fry over high heat for 2¹/₂-3 minutes. Add the sesame oil and sugar and stir-fry for a further 2 minutes. Return the vegetables to the pork and continue stir-frying for 1 minute.

Serve immediately, with rice or noodles.

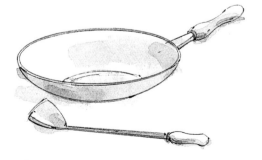

Pork

Spiced orange spare ribs

(pictured page 61)

Orange juice, lemon juice, Worcestershire sauce and honey combine to give the ribs a delicious sweet spicy flavour whilst, at the same time, imparting a handsome glaze.

Serves 4

1.25kg (3 lb) lean spare ribs

Marinade:

2 tablespoons clear honey

juice of ¹/₂ lemon

grated zest of ¹/₂ and juice of 2 oranges

2 tablespoons Worcestershire sauce

2 teaspoons soy sauce

salt

Mix together the marinade ingredients in a pan and heat gently. Simmer for 2 minutes and allow to cool.

If the ribs are in whole slabs, cut into sections of three or four ribs. Place the ribs, together with the marinade, in a plastic bag and securely close with a twist-tie. Put the bag in a roasting pan or similar dish (in case of leakage) and refrigerate for 12-24 hours, turning over the bag occasionally.

Prepare the barbecue for grilling, following the instructions on page 8.

Briefly drain the spare ribs and reserve the marinade. Cook the ribs, over medium heat, for about 1¹/₄ hours* or until the meat has pulled away from the rib ends exposing 1-2cm (¹/₂-³/₄ inch) of bone. Turn the ribs frequently during the cooking time, but baste occasionally only during the final 15 minutes so the surface of the ribs doesn't become charred. When properly cooked the spare ribs will have a deep golden, semi-translucent appearance and the meat will be tender and juicy.

* If the ribs are 'mean on meat', the cooking time given can be reduced considerably.

Indonesian pork satay with peanut sauce

The orange, mint and ginger marinade gives the lamb a fresh, slightly sharp, flavour.

Serves 4

1.1kg (2¹/₂ lb) boneless pork loin

3 tablespoons soy sauce

3 tablespoons groundnut oil, plus extra for basting

1 tablespoon chopped onion

1 garlic clove, crushed

1 teaspoon sugar

a pinch of mild curry powder

Peanut sauce:

50g (2oz) shredded coconut flesh

150ml (¹/₄ pint) hot milk

2 tablespoons soft butter

¹/₂ teaspoon mild curry powder

¹/₂ teaspoon freshly grated root ginger

1 garlic clove, chopped very finely

1 medium-size onion, chopped finely

50g (2oz) crushed pineapple

150ml (¹/₄ pint) chicken stock

2 tablespoons sugar

3 tablespoons smooth peanut butter

¹/₂ teaspoon salt

a pinch of freshly ground black pepper

Cut the pork into 2.5cm x 10cm x 5mm (1 x 4 x ¹/₄ inch) strips. Soak bamboo skewers in water, if using.

Combine the soy sauce, oil, onion, garlic, sugar and curry powder. Marinate the meat strips in the mixture, in the refrigerator, for 2-3 hours, stirring occasionally.

Meanwhile, make the sauce. Soak the shredded coconut in the milk for about 30 minutes. Then melt the butter in an ovenproof dish or deep frying pan, add the curry powder and cook, over fairly gentle heat, for 1 minute. Add the ginger, garlic and onion and continue to cook for 5 minutes. Add the soaked coconut and milk, pineapple, chicken stock, sugar and peanut butter. Season to taste with the salt and pepper and cook for 15-20 minutes, stirring occasionally.

Prepare the barbecue for grilling, following the instructions on page 8.

Drain the meat and thread on to thin metal skewers or soaked bamboo sticks. Cook, over medium to high heat, for 5-10 minutes. Turn and baste frequently with groundnut oil.

Serve the meat with the peanut sauce.

Pork

Lemony pork chops

Serves 4

4 loin or chump chops, cut 2.5cm (1 inch) thick

Marinade:

Juice and grated zest of 1 lemon

4 bay leaves

4 tablespoons oil

1 tablespoon chopped fresh parsley

a pinch of dried oregano

a pinch of dried thyme

a pinch of dried sage

a pinch of salt

$^1/_4$ teaspoon freshly ground black pepper

1 garlic clove, crushed

Wipe the chops and slash the fat around the edge of each at 1cm ($^1/_2$ inch) intervals.

Combine the marinade ingredients.

Place the chops in a shallow dish and spoon the marinade over the meat. Cover the dish and refrigerate for 6-24 hours, turning the chops over once or twice.

Prepare the barbecue for grilling, following the instructions on page 8.

Reserving the marinade, remove the chops and place on the grill. Cook, over medium to high heat, for 15-20 minutes each side or until all the pink colour in the centre of the meat has disappeared. Baste the chops occasionally with the marinade during cooking.

Hot and spicy pork steaks

Serves 4

4 pork shoulder steaks

Marinade:

2 teaspoons wholegrain mustard

1 teaspoon paprika

1 garlic clove, crushed

1 fresh green chilli, finely chopped

2-3 drops Tabasco

4 tablespoons white wine vinegar

4 tablespoons olive oil

salt and freshly ground black pepper

Combine the marinade ingredients. Place the pork steaks in a shallow dish and spoon over the marinade. Cover the dish and allow to marinate for 2 hours.

Prepare the barbecue for grilling, following the instructions on page 8.

Reserving the marinade, remove the steaks and place on the grill. Cook over medium to high heat, for 15-20 minutes or until all the pink colour in the centre of the meat has disappeared. Baste the steaks with the reserved marinade during the final few minutes of cooking.

Pictured opposite:
Soy-glazed roast loin of pork
Roast loin of pork with ambrosia stuffing
Spiced orange spare ribs

Pork

Stir-fried pork with oyster sauce

Serves 4

250g (8oz) lean pork, preferably tenderloin

250g (8oz) spinach

3 tablespoons vegetable oil

$^1/_2$ teaspoon salt

$^1/_4$ teaspoon sugar

1 tablespoon water

2 tablespoons oyster sauce

6 baby corns, broken into small pieces

$^1/_2$ teaspoon sesame oil

freshly ground black pepper

Marinade:

$^1/_2$ teaspoon soy sauce

$^1/_2$ teaspoon sesame oil

1 teaspoon rice wine or dry sherry

$^1/_2$ teaspoon sugar

1 egg yolk

1 tablespoon cornflour

salt and freshly ground black pepper

Prepare the barbecue for wok-cooking, following the instructions on page 14.

Slice the pork into bite-size pieces.

For the marinade, combine the soy sauce, sesame oil, rice wine or sherry, sugar, egg yolk and salt and pepper to taste and mix well. Stir the pork into this mixture and marinate for about 10 minutes. Stir in the cornflour just before cooking.

Cut the spinach into 5cm (2 inch) pieces. Position the wok on the barbecue and heat 1 tablespoon of the vegetable oil. Add the salt and the spinach and stir-fry quickly over high heat. Add the sugar and water and stir again. Drain the liquid from the wok, remove the spinach and keep warm.

Heat the remaining vegetable oil in the wok and stir-fry the pork until golden brown all over. Remove the pork from the wok and keep warm.

Add the oyster sauce to the wok and when the liquid begins to bubble, return the pork pieces to it and stir-fry for about a minute. Return the spinach and add the baby corn pieces. Sprinkle with the sesame oil and black pepper to taste and stir for another minute or so.

Serve immediately.

Roast loin of pork with ambrosia stuffing

(pictured page 61)

Serves 6-8

1.75kg (4 lb) loin of pork, boned and rolled

Ambrosia stuffing:

3 tablespoons soft butter, plus 3 tablespoons melted butter

2 medium-size onions, chopped

2 medium-size cooking or eating apples, cored, peeled and chopped

175g (6oz) ripe olives, stoned and chopped

75g (3oz) walnuts, chopped

¹/₄ teaspoon dried thyme

¹/₂ teaspoon salt

75g (3oz) fresh breadcrumbs

75g (3oz) cooked ham, chopped

Prepare the barbecue for 'Indirect heat' cooking, following the instructions on page 10.

Using a sharp knife, slice the loin halfway down at 2.5cm (1 inch) intervals. Then cut down further into each incision to form deep pockets, taking care to leave a 2.5cm (1 inch) wall on the sides and bottom of the loin roll.

To make the stuffing, heat the soft butter in a skillet or pan and cook the onions, stirring occasionally, until transparent. Add the apples and continue cooking for 1 minute. Add the olives, walnuts, thyme, salt, breadcrumbs, melted butter and ham and mix well.

Fill each pocket in the meat generously with the stuffing. Tie the roll lengthways at 2.5cm (1 inch) intervals to hold it firmly together.

Roast, with medium to high heat, for about 1¹/₂-2 hours until the meat is well done. A meat thermometer buried in the centre of the roast should register 85°C/185°F.

Remove the roast from the barbecue and allow to stand for about 10 minutes before carving. Remove the string and slice through the meat between the pockets to make individually stuffed portions.

Sally Ducker's Caribbean Roast

Serves 3–4

'Caribbean Rub':

1 tablespoon brown sugar

2 teaspoons ground allspice

2 teaspoons onion powder

$^1/_2$ teaspoon dried thyme

1 teaspoon salt

$^1/_2$ teaspoon ground nutmeg

1 tablespoon dark rum

1-1$^1/_4$kg (2-3 lb) pork rib roast

Mango Sauce:

1 mango, chopped

$^1/_2$ medium chopped onion

2 tablespoons mango chutney

2-3 tablespoons dark rum

1oz butter

2 tablespoons cream of coconut

1 teaspoon 'Caribbean rub'

125ml (4floz) chicken stock

salt to taste

freshly ground black pepper

The night before you plan to barbecue, combine the rub ingredients in a small bowl. Massage the pork well with the rum and then with about half of the rub. Transfer the pork to a plastic bag, or food wrap, and refrigerate overnight.

Prepare the 'Pit barbecue' (Smoker) for barbecuing or, alternately, if using a lidded charcoal or gas barbecue, prepare it for 'smoke-cooking by following the instructions for the 'Indirect heat' cooking technique set out on page 10. Whichever of the above barbecues you are using, bring its cooking temperature to a low 100-120°C.

Remove the pork from the refrigerator. Pat down the pork lightly with another coating of rub. Let the meat sit at room temperature for 30-40 minutes before transferring it to the smoker, or covered barbecue, fattier side up. Cook for 4$^1/_2$–5 hours.

Whist the roast cooks, prepare the sauce. In a food processor or blender, purée together the mango, onion and chutney, pouring in some of the stock if a little thick. Spoon the mixture into a heavy-based saucepan and add the remaining stock, rum, cream of coconut and Caribbean rub. Warm the mixture over a medium heat and simmer for about 20 minutes. Taste, and add as much salt and freshly ground black pepper as necessary to balance the savoury and sweet flavours. The sauce can be kept warm, or refrigerated and then reheated, when the meat is ready for consumption. The butter should be added to the warm sauce just before serving.

Having removed the pork from the smoker, or barbecue, let it sit at room temperature for 10-15 minutes before carving.

Serve, accompanied by the warm sauce.

Sally's tip

To regulate the smoke flavour, wrap the meat in foil during part of the cooking process.

Spicy pork chops

The delicious spicy flavour and attractive appearance, comes from a combination of Dijon mustard, soy sauce, chilli powder and honey.

Serves 6

6 pork loin chops, 2.5cm (1 inch) thick

6 tablespoons clear honey

6 tablespoons Dijon mustard

2 tablespoons soy sauce

$1/4$ teaspoon chilli powder

$1/2$ teaspoon salt

Wipe the chops and slash the fat around the edge of each at 1cm ($1/2$ inch) intervals.

Mix together the honey, mustard, soy sauce, chilli powder and salt in a shallow dish.

Place the chops in the dish and spoon over the marinade. Cover the dish and refrigerate for 6-24 hours, turning the chops over once or twice.

Prepare the barbecue for grilling, following the instructions on page 8.

Reserving the marinade, remove the chops and place on the grill. Cook, over medium to high heat, for 15-20 minutes each side or until all the pink colour in the centre of the meat has disappeared. Baste the chops with the marinade just before turning and during the final few minutes of cooking.

Grilled gammon steaks with spicy apple sauce

Serves 4

3 tablespoons apple sauce

2 tablespoons orange juice

1 teaspoon grated orange zest

2 teaspoons Dijon mustard

a pinch of dried thyme

a pinch of dried sage

4 gammon steaks

Prepare the barbecue for grilling, following the instructions on page 8.

Mix together the apple sauce, orange juice and zest, and stir in the mustard, thyme and sage.

Brush the apple mixture over one side of the gammon steaks. Grill the coated side, over medium heat, for about 3 minutes.

Brush the top of the steaks with more mixture, turn over and grill for a further 3 minutes. Continue brushing and turning the steaks until done.

Serve immediately, with some additional apple sauce and mustard.

Pork

Oriental pork belly

Despite its suggestive title, Oriental Pork Belly tastes yummy, hot or cold, and, appropriately, (shape-wise), goes well with jacket potatoes.

Serves 6-8

1.25kg (3 lb) belly of pork on the bone
Marinade:

1 garlic clove

¹/₂ teaspoon salt

3 tablespoons soy sauce

4 tablespoons clear honey

¹/₂ teaspoon ground cinnamon

Using a sharp knife, carefully remove the rind from the pork, leaving the fat intact.

Score the fat to leave a diamond pattern.

Crush the garlic clove and salt together in a pestle and mortar (or use a spoon and a saucer). Mix the garlic, soy sauce, honey and cinnamon in a shallow dish.

Place the pork, skin side down, in the marinade. Cover the dish and refrigerate for 6-24 hours. Remove the dish from the refrigerator an hour or so before the meat is cooked to allow the meat to reach room temperature.

Prepare the barbecue for 'Indirect heat' cooking, following the instructions on page 10.

Half-fill a roasting tin with hot water and cover with a wire rack. Place the roasting tin on the unlit side of the barbecue.

Remove the meat from the marinade, reserving the marinade. Place the meat, skin side down, in the centre of the wire rack. Cook, with medium heat, for 1 hour. Turn the meat over and baste with the remaining marinade. Cook the meat for a further 1 hour.

Cut the pork into thin slices down to the bone.

Spicy glazed baked ham

Serves 25-30

**5-6kg (12-14 lb) boneless
cooked gammon**

4 tablespoons oyster sauce

2 tablespoons dry sherry

2-3 tablespoons whole cloves

Preheat and prepare the barbecue for 'Indirect heat' cooking, following the instructions on page 10.

Using a sharp knife, cut through the rind (to the fat) down the middle of the gammon and around its circumference. Position the ham on the barbecue and cook, at medium heat, for 30-40 minutes or until the rind down the middle moves apart by 2.5cm (1 inch) or so. Pull the rind away from the ham and score the fat in a diamond pattern.

Combine the oyster sauce and dry sherry. Rub the scored surface of the ham with the mixture and stick a single clove into the centre of each diamond. If you have a meat thermometer available insert this into the heart of the ham and continue cooking, with the lid down, at medium heat for a further 2 hours or so or until the thermometer registers 85°C/185°F. If you do not have a meat thermometer allow 8-10 minutes per 500g (1 lb). Avoid cooking the ham at too high a temperature.

Note: As an alternative to the above glaze, try using orange marmalade or a mixture of brown sugar, mustard powder and pineapple syrup.

Soy-glazed roast loin of pork

(pictured page 61)

The combination of soy sauce, apple juice, garlic and ginger on the skin of the loin produces a dark and handsome glaze. For those who like the crisp, tasty crackling, serve the meat with a strip or two, and an extra serviette. This dish is equally delicious when served hot or cold.

Serves 6-8

125ml (4floz) apple juice

3 tablespoons soy sauce

1 garlic clove, chopped very finely

**1 teaspoon freshly grated root ginger or
$^1/_4$ teaspoon ground ginger**

1.75kg (4 lb) loin of pork

Prepare the barbecue for 'Indirect heat' cooking, following the instructions on page 10. (Use a drip pan.)

Mix together the apple juice, soy sauce, garlic and ginger and place on one side.

With a sharp, short-bladed knife eg. a Stanley knife, score the skin of the loin at roughly 1cm ($^1/_2$ inch) intervals.

Roast the loin, fat side up, with medium heat for 1 hour. Generously baste the scored skin with the marinade. Cook the meat for a further 1$^1/_2$ hours or until the meat is well done (a meat thermometer inserted into the thickest part should register 85°C/185°F). Baste frequently during the final 20-30 minutes of cooking to produce an attractive dark glaze.

The juices collected in the drip pan will make a rich and very tasty gravy.

Pork

Stir-fried pork with pineapple

Serves 4

500g (1 lb) lean pork, preferably tenderloin, cut into thin strips

4 tablespoons vegetable oil

1 large onion, coarsely chopped

1 green pepper, de-seeded and cut into 2cm (³/₄ inch) squares

1 teaspoon finely grated fresh root ginger or ¹/₄ teaspoon ground ginger

3 tablespoons soy sauce

1 tablespoon dry sherry or sake

1 tablespoon red wine vinegar

¹/₄ teaspoon salt

¹/₂ teaspoon sugar

250g (8oz) tin pineapple chunks, with the juice reserved

250g (8oz) tin water chestnuts, drained and sliced

2 level tablespoons cornflour, blended with 3 tablespoons cold water

Prepare the barbecue for wok-cooking, following the instructions on page 14. Stir-fry the pork in 2 tablespoons of the oil for about 5 minutes. Remove from the wok and hold to one side of the grill. Add the remaining oil to the wok and stir--fry the onion and green pepper for about 2 minutes. Return the pork to the wok and stir in the soy sauce, sherry, red wine vinegar, salt and sugar. Add the pineapple chunks and make up the reserved juice to 300ml (¹/₂ pint) with water. Add the diluted juice to the wok along with the water chestnuts. Stir in the blended cornflour and stir-fry for 2-3 minutes.

Garlic and gingered spare ribs

Serves around 6

2.75kg (6 lb) lean spare ribs

Marinade:

4 garlic cloves, chopped very finely

2 tablespoons preserved ginger, chopped finely

275ml (9floz) chicken stock

125g (4oz) orange marmalade

3 tablespoons red wine vinegar

3 tablespoons tomato ketchup

2 teaspoons soy sauce

Mix together the garlic, ginger, stock, marmalade, vinegar, ketchup and soy sauce to make a marinade.

Place a large plastic bag in a roasting pan or large dish. If the ribs are in whole slabs, cut them into three or four rib sections. Put the ribs in the bag and pour in the marinade. Securely close the bag with a twist-tie.

Place the tin or dish in the refrigerator and leave for 12-24 hours, turning the bag occasionally.

Prepare the barbecue for grilling, following the instructions on page 8.

Remove the ribs from the marinade and drain briefly, reserving the marinade.

Cook, over medium heat, for about 1¹/₄ hours or until the meat pulls away from the end of the rib bones. Turn the ribs frequently but baste only occasionally, and not too liberally, with the reserved marinade.

Serve immediately accompanied, I suggest, with boiled rice.

Five-Spice spare ribs

The rich, delicious blend of Chinese Five-Spice seasoning and sumptuous sauces in this recipe, will ensure that there will be no spare, spare ribs, left over from the cook-out....only some bones in remarkable pristine condition !

Serves 2-4

1.25kg (3 lb) meaty spare ribs

Marinade:

1 tablespoon rice wine or dry sherry

1 tablespoon oyster sauce

4 tablespoons Hoisin sauce

50g (2oz) sugar

$1/2$ teaspoon Five-Spice seasoning

Mix together the marinade ingredients.

If the ribs are in whole slabs, cut into three or four rib sections. Place the ribs, together with the marinade, in a strong plastic bag and securely close the bag with a twist-tie. Put the bag in a dish (in case of leakage) and refrigerate for 12-24 hours, turning the bag over occasionally.

Prepare the barbecue for grilling, following the instructions on page 8.

Remove the ribs from the marinade and drain briefly, reserving the marinade. Cook the ribs, over medium heat, for about $1^1/2$ hours or until the meat has pulled away from the end of the rib ends exposing 1-2cm ($1/2$-$3/4$ inch) of bone.

Turn the ribs frequently, basting two or three times with the reserved marinade during the final 10-15 minutes of cooking.

Serve with a roll of kitchen towelling!

Piquant pork steaks

Serves 4

4 pork shoulder steaks,
cut 2.5cm (1 inch) thick

Marinade:

4 tablespoons white wine vinegar

4 tablespoons oil

2 teaspoons wholegrain mustard

1 tablespoon soy sauce

2 garlic cloves, crushed

1 fresh green chilli, chopped very finely

1 teaspoon paprika

a few drops of Tabasco

salt and freshly ground black pepper

Wipe steaks and place in a shallow dish. Combine the marinade ingredients and spoon over the steaks.

Cover the dish and allow to marinate in the refrigerator for 2-8 hours.

Prepare the barbecue for grilling, following the instructions on page 8.

Reserving the marinade, remove the steaks and place on the grill. Cook, over medium to high heat, for 15-20 minutes each side or until all the pink colour in the centre of the meat has disappeared. Baste the steaks with the reserved marinade during cooking.

Pork

Baked ham with brown sugar glaze

(pictured opposite)

2.25kg (5 lb) piece of middle cut gammon, rolled

750ml (1¹/₂ pints) dry cider

1 medium-size onion, stuck with 6-10 cloves

2 bay leaves

6 black peppercorns

about 36 cloves

Brown sugar glaze:

125g (4oz) brown sugar

¹/₂ teaspoon ground cinnamon

1 tablespoon English mustard

4 tablespoons beer, cider or cranberry, apple or orange juice

Soak the gammon in cold water for a few hours (change the water during this period). Remove the joint and place in a saucepan or casserole that will accommodate it comfortably.

Pour over 600ml (1 pint) of the cider plus enough cold water to cover the gammon completely. Add the onion, bay leaves and peppercorns, bring to the boil and simmer gently for 1 hour.

Drain the gammon, let it cool a little, remove the string and carefully cut off the skin. Stand the gammon, fat side uppermost, in a roasting tin. Pour the remainder of the cider into the tin. Lightly score the fat in diagonal lines (about 2.5cm/1 inch apart) in different directions to form diamond shapes.

Prepare the barbecue for 'Indirect heat' cooking, following the instructions on page 10.

Combine the sugar, cinnamon, mustard and beer, cider or fruit juice in a small saucepan and heat gently until the sugar has dissolved. Brush the glaze mixture all over the joint. Insert a clove in the centre of each diamond shape.

Bake the gammon, with medium heat, for 1-1¹/₄ hours, basting occasionally with the cider enriched juices.

Pictured opposite:
Baked ham with brown sugar glaze
Roasted potatoes with garlic, rosemary and thyme

Redskin wild duck

Although game butchers will supply the ducks well hung and ready to cook, they still need to be carefully wiped, inside and out, with a slightly damp cloth just before cooking.

Serves 4-8

4 wild ducks each weighing 500g-1.1kg (1-2$^1/_2$ lb) well hung

125g (4oz) butter, softened

Worcestershire sauce for coating

paprika for sprinkling

1$^1/_2$ tablespoons cornflour

3 tablespoons port

Prepare the barbecue for 'Indirect heat' cooking, following the instructions on page 10.

Lightly rub the entire body of each duck with the butter. Place the ducks, head to tail, on a trivet (a cake rack will do) which has been set in a roasting tin. The tin should be of a size to sit comfortably on just one half of the barbecue's grill area if your unit is gas-fired. Apply several shots of Worcestershire sauce over each duck and then sprinkle with sufficient paprika to completely coat the birds' breasts and legs.

Cook, with medium to high heat, until the ducks are cooked to the desired degree. Depending on the weight of the individual ducks, and the way you like them cooked, this could take 25-75 minutes.

Remove the ducks and let them stand (or sit) for a few minutes. If they are large, cut them in half with poultry shears, or heavy duty kitchen scissors, to double up the servings. Remove the trivet or rack from the roasting tin and carefully spoon off all the fat.

To make the gravy, blend the cornflour with the port and add to the tin juices. Place the tin over the barbecue's fire-bed and bring the gravy to the boil, stirring constantly. Boil and stir for a minute or so before spooning some of the rich sauce over the duck portions. Serve the remaining sauce in a warmed sauce-boat.

Roast chicken with 'Puts'
(Pesto under the skin)

(pictured on page 121)

In terms of vision and taste, this is a roast chicken with a difference. Inserting Pesto under the skin is not difficult unless, that is, one's fingernails are perhaps excessively long and sharp. The skin of most chickens is fairly tough, yet remarkably supple and stretchy. Apart from the ridge of the breastbone (where you might have to gently use a short bladed knife) and the knuckle ends of the drumsticks, the thin membrane that connects the skin to the flesh of the chicken is easily parted by gently working your fingers between them. Try to avoid breaking through the skin if you can, but the odd little tear is quite all right.

Serves 4-6

1.25-1.75kg (3-4 lb) chicken (select one with its skin nicely intact)

Pesto:

**3 tablespoons pine nuts
or toasted hazelnuts**

**2 tablespoons freshly grated
parmesan cheese**

a loose handful of fresh basil leaves

2 garlic cloves, peeled

2 tablespoons olive oil

1 egg yolk (optional)

50g (2oz) medium-fat soft cheese

salt and freshly ground black pepper

groundnut oil

parmesan

To make the Pesto, place the pine nuts (or toasted hazelnuts), parmesan, garlic cloves and basil leaves in a food processor, or blender. Process for about 20 seconds or so, then add the olive oil and egg yolk, if using. Continue processing until the mixture resembles a rough paste. Add the soft cheese and seasoning, then pulse (a few quick bursts of the processor) until the mixture blends together.

Using your hand, spread the Pesto evenly under the skin and over the meat.

Brush the chicken with the groundnut oil.

Prepare the barbecue for 'Indirect heat' cooking, following the instructions on page 10.

Roast the chicken, with medium to high heat, for about 1½ hours or until the juices run clear when the chicken thigh is pierced with a skewer.

Scattering a little grated parmesan over the oiled surface of the chicken after roughly an hour into cooking will produce an attractive light golden crust over the bird.

Note: If in a hurry, purchase a jar of the excellent, freshly prepared, Pesto stocked by many of the larger super-markets - adding perhaps some extra ground pine nuts or ground toasted hazelnuts to give the Pesto more body.

PoultryandGame

Chicken with chilli glaze

As barbecue cooks our primary aim should be to produce food, be it a sausage or a steak, with the maximum possible appeal to all the senses, particularly sight and smell. Stimulating your guests taste buds well before they get their teeth into the food will have a positive and beneficial effect on their appetites This colourful, red-glazed chicken does just that and tastes good too!

Serves 4

4 tablespoons melted butter

1 teaspoon chilli powder

2 garlic cloves, chopped very finely

2 tablespoons lime juice

$1/4$ teaspoon grated lime zest

$1/4$ teaspoon ground cumin

1.25kg (3 lb) chicken, jointed

Prepare the barbecue for grilling, following the instructions on page 8.

Mix together the butter, chilli powder, garlic, lime juice and zest and cumin. Generously brush the chicken pieces with the mixture.

Place the chicken pieces, skin side up, on the grill and grill over medium to high heat for about 40 minutes, turning the pieces and basting frequently, until the meat is cooked.

Chicken satay with Indonesian sauce

Serves 4

Ingredients for 1 quantity of Indonesian sauce (page 158)

750g (1$1/2$ lb) chicken breasts, boned and skinned

groundnut oil for brushing

Marinade:

1 garlic clove, crushed

2 tablespoons soy sauce

juice of 1 lemon

To Serve:

shredded lettuce

Prepare the Indonesian Sauce 2 or 3 hours before cooking the chicken, following the instructions on page 158. Soak some skewers in water if using bamboo.

Cut the meat into 2.5cm (1 inch) cubes. Mix together the marinade ingredients in a bowl and add the chicken cubes, turning to coat with the mixture. Cover the bowl and leave to marinate for about 30 minutes.

Prepare the barbecue for grilling, following the instructions on page 8.

Remove the meat from the marinade and thread them on to soaked bamboo or metal skewers. Reheat the sauce gently, adding a little water if it is too thick. Brush the meat with a little oil and grill, over medium heat, for about 6-8 minutes or until the meat is cooked.

Serve the chicken on a dish lined with shredded lettuce and accompanied by the Indonesian Sauce.

Honsoywin chicken quarters

A very tasty dish to set before your guests, but take care not to over-baste as this could make the skin overly dark and burnt. Aim for a deep golden 'mahogany' hue with a nicely lacquered 'overcoat'.

Serves 4

Marinade:

4 tablespoons clear honey

4 tablespoons soy sauce

150ml ('/4 pint) white wine

150ml ('/4 pint) orange juice

'/4 teaspoon ground allspice

1 teaspoon paprika

1 garlic clove, crushed

2 tablespoons water

Place the chicken quarters in a dish.

To make the marinade, mix together all the ingredients. Pour the marinade over the chicken quarters, turning them to ensure an even coating. Cover the dish and leave in the refrigerator for a few hours or overnight; turn the pieces occasionally during this time.

Prepare the barbecue for grilling, following the instructions on page 8.

Drain the chicken pieces, reserving the marinade, and place on the grill. Cook, over medium heat, for 40-50 minutes or until fully cooked, basting with the marinade several times. To check if each quarter is cooked, pierce the thickest part with a skewer - the juices should run clear. If in any doubt, cut the meat to the bone, in the thickest part, and check to see that the meat next to the bone is no longer pink.

'Quick-chick' Tikka Masala kebabs

A great looking, delicious, 'fast-track' dish.

Serves 4

750g (1'/2 lb) chicken breasts, boned and skinned

Marinade:

4 tablespoons Tikka Masala curry paste

150g (5oz) carton natural yoghurt

salt and freshly ground black pepper

To serve:

pitta bread

Cut each chicken breast into 5 or 6 pieces. Mix the curry paste with the yoghurt in a bowl and add the chicken pieces. Leave to marinate for about 30 minutes.

In the meantime prepare the barbecue for grilling, following the instructions on page 8.

Thread the chicken onto soaked bamboo or metal skewers and season with salt and pepper. Place on the grill, or greased griddle plate, and cook, over medium heat, for 10-15 minutes or until the chicken is cooked through and beginning to char around the edges.

Serve the chicken with the pitta bread accompanied by a refreshing cucumber or apple dip.

Orange burgundy duckling

(pictured page 87)

Serves 4

1.75-2.25kg (4-5 lb) duckling

300ml ($\frac{1}{2}$ pint) Burgundy wine
(red or white)

1 teaspoon salt

1 teaspoon freshly ground black pepper

$\frac{1}{2}$ teaspoon dried thyme

1 orange, quartered

2 slices of onion

1 celery top

150ml ($\frac{1}{4}$ pint) concentrated orange
juice

Garnish:

thinly sliced oranges

Prepare the barbecue for 'Indirect heat'
cooking, following the instructions on page
10. (Use a drip pan.)

Remove any giblets from the duckling. Wash
and pat dry, inside and out, with kitchen
paper.

Brush the cavity of the duckling with a little of
the burgundy and sprinkle with the salt,
pepper and thyme. Place the orange, onion
and celery inside and close the cavity with fine
skewers.

Mix together the remaining burgundy and the
orange juice and use it to brush the outside of
the duckling.

Roast the duckling with medium to high heat
for about 2 hours or until tender, occasionally
pricking the thigh and breast skin with a fine,
sharp-pointed skewer or large needle and
basting with the wine mixture after 30
minutes. Baste frequently during cooking.

Discard the flavourings in the cavity and cut
the duckling into portions. Place them on a
hot serving dish. If desired, skim the fat from
the pan juices and pour the juices over the
portions. Arrange orange slices around the
edge of the dish.

Stir-fried 5-spice chicken with lemon grass and several etc's

Serves 4-5

625g (1½ lb) chicken breasts, boned, skinned and sliced thinly

50g (2oz) finely chopped lemon grass

2 teaspoons grated fresh root ginger

2 garlic cloves, crushed

1½ tablespoons lime juice

1 teaspoon zest of lime

1 teaspoon 5-spice powder

60ml (2floz) soy sauce

2 tablespoons groundnut oil

250g (8oz) Chinese lettuce, shredded

125 (4oz) bean sprouts

8 spring onions, sliced

½ handful fresh coriander leaves

Combine the chicken, lemon grass, ginger, garlic, lime juice, 5-spice and 1 tablespoon of the soy sauce in a large bowl. Cover the bowl and keep in a cool place for 3-4 hours or overnight in the refrigerator.

Prepare the barbecue for wok-cooking, following the instructions on page 14.

Place the wok on the barbecue and heat 1 tablespoon of the oil. Stir-fry the chicken mixture in small batches until all has been well browned and cooked through. Keep the cooked chicken in a dish adjacent to the barbecue to keep warm.

Heat the remaining oil and stir-fry the lettuce, onion and bean sprouts until the lettuce just begins to wilt.

Return the chicken mixture to the wok, along with the coriander and remainder of the soy sauce, and toss all together to mix well.

Serving suggestion:

Serve on a bed of fine Chinese egg noodles.

Teriyaki turkey drumsticks

If unable to buy small drumsticks (it appears easier to purchase turkey drumsticks that are more akin in size to small legs of lamb), part-cook the larger drumsticks in the barbecue using the 'Indirect heat' method (page 10) or in the kitchen oven, before finishing them off on the grill.

Serves 6

6 small turkey drumsticks

Marinade:

150ml ('/4 pint) soy sauce

4 tablespoons clear honey

3 tablespoons mirin or dry sherry

2 teaspoons freshly grated root ginger or '/2 teaspoon ground ginger

150ml ('/4 pint) oil

2 garlic cloves, crushed

50g (2oz) spring onion, sliced thinly

Wash the drumsticks, pat dry and pierce all over with the point of a skewer. Combine all the marinade ingredients and mix well. Pour over the drumsticks, turning them to make sure they are well coated. Cover the dish and leave in the refrigerator for a few hours or overnight. Turn the drumsticks occasionally while they are in the marinade.

Prepare the barbecue for grilling, following the instructions on page 8.

Briefly drain the drumsticks (reserve the marinade) and place on the grill. Cook the drumsticks over medium to high heat for about 40-50 minutes or until cooked, turning and basting frequently with the marinade. To check if they are cooked, pierce the thickest part with a skewer - the juices should run clear. If in doubt, cut the meat in the same area and look to see that the meat is no longer pink.

Tandoori chicken

In spite of the number of spices in this recipe, the end result is fairly mild. Excellent bottled tandoori paste is available in all supermarkets if you don't have the time, or feel inclined, to make your own.

Serves 6-8

3 x 1kg (2 lb) fresh chickens

juice of 1¹/₂ lemons

melted ghee, or groundnut oil, for brushing

Tandoori marinade:

4 medium-size garlic cloves

1cm (¹/₂ inch) piece of fresh root ginger peeled and chopped

1 teaspoon ground roasted cumin seeds

¹/₂ teaspoon ground cardamom

¹/₂ teaspoon ground cinnamon

¹/₄ teaspoon ground nutmeg

¹/₂ teaspoon chilli powder

¹/₂ teaspoon cayenne pepper

1 teaspoon salt

125ml (4floz) natural yoghurt

Cut the chicken into quarters and remove the wings from the breast pieces. Pull the skin from all the quarters (kitchen paper will help provide a better grip); then pierce the flesh all over with the point of a skewer or a sharp-pointed kitchen fork. Make deep diagonal slashes in the meat about 2.5cm (1 inch) apart.

Place the portions in a large bowl. Sprinkle over the lemon juice and rub in well for a minute or two. Cover the bowl and leave for 30 minutes.

For the tandoori marinade, put all the ingredients in a food processor or blender and blend until the mixture is smooth. Pour the marinade over the chicken portions and mix thoroughly to coat well. Cover the bowl again and leave the chicken to marinate for at least 4 hours or overnight in the refrigerator. Remove the bowl from the refrigerator at least 1 hour before cooking to allow the chicken to come to room temperature.

Prepare the barbecue for grilling, following the instructions on page 8.

Place the chicken portions on the grill, bone side down, and brush the slashed surface of the meat with melted ghee or oil. Cook, over medium to high heat, for about 10 minutes. Turn and baste the other side and cook for a further 10 minutes. Continue to cook, turning and basting the chicken every 10 minutes or until the meat is cooked - this will take 30-40 minutes.

Serve the chicken with lemon wedges and a salad.

Sesame gingered chicken

Serves 4

8 chicken thighs or drumsticks

Marinade:

2.5cm (1 inch) piece of fresh root ginger, peeled and grated

2 tablespoons sesame seeds

2 teaspoons sesame oil

1 tablespoon groundnut oil

1 garlic clove, chopped very finely

$^1/_4$ teaspoon cayenne pepper

25g (1oz) spring onion, chopped finely

Wash the chicken thighs or drumsticks, pat dry and pierce all over with the point of a skewer.

Combine the marinade ingredients and mix thoroughly. Brush the marinade all over the thighs or drumsticks and place in a dish. Cover the dish and leave in the refrigerator for a few hours or overnight.

Prepare the barbecue for grilling, following the instructions on page 8.

Lightly drain the thighs or drumsticks, reserving any marinade. Grill, over medium to high heat, for about 30 minutes or until nicely browned and cooked, turning and basting with the marinade a few times during cooking.

Grilled poussins with mustard

If you can't obtain poussins, very small chickens, about 375g (12oz) in weight, may be used instead.

Serves 4

4 poussins

125ml (4floz) groundnut oil

1 tablespoon French mustard

1 teaspoon dried rosemary

1 teaspoon dried thyme

2 bay leaves, crushed

dry white breadcrumbs for sprinkling

salt and freshly ground black pepper

Prepare the barbecue for grilling, following the instructions on page 8.

Split the poussins in half, from the back. Open them out and gently crush the bones by pressing down with the heel of your hand (or use a large heavy-bladed knife or cleaver) so that they lie flat whilst cooking. Season the poussins.

Combine the oil, mustard, rosemary, thyme and bay leaves and mix well.

Brush some of the mixture over the poussins and grill them, bone side down, over medium to high heat, for about 10 minutes. Turn and grill the other side for 10-15 minutes or until cooked.

Brush the rest of the mustard mixture over the poussins and scatter with breadcrumbs. Return the poussins to the grill and cook for a further 2-3 minutes or until nicely browned.

Sweet and sour chicken

Serves 4

1.25-1.5kg (3-3$\frac{1}{2}$ lb) chicken

150ml ($\frac{1}{4}$ pint) soy sauce

200g (7oz) can of pineapple chunks

150ml ($\frac{1}{4}$ pint) chicken stock

2 garlic cloves, chopped very finely

1 tablespoon freshly grated root ginger
or 1 teaspoon ground ginger

50g (2oz) brown sugar

3 tablespoons red or white wine vinegar

1 green pepper, de-seeded and cut into
2.5cm (1 inch) squares

1 firm, ripe tomato, skinned, de-seeded
and chopped

4 spring onions, sliced diagonally into
2.5cm (1 inch) pieces

2 tablespoons cornflour

3 tablespoons cold water

Using a heavy kitchen cleaver, joint and chop the chicken into 5cm (2 inch) pieces.

Combine the soy sauce, the pineapple juice from the can, the chicken stock, garlic, ginger, brown sugar and vinegar and mix well. Marinate the chicken pieces in the mixture, in a cool place, for 2-3 hours. Remove the chicken pieces from the marinade about 30 minutes before cooking. Reserve the marinade.

Prepare the barbecue for 'Indirect heat' cooking, following the instructions on page 10.

Brown the chicken pieces for about 15 minutes over the lit side of the barbecue. Transfer the part-cooked chicken to a deep-sided roasting tin. Arrange the pepper, tomato, pineapple chunks and spring onions around the chicken pieces and pour the reserved marinade over. Position the roasting tin over the unlit side of the barbecue and cook, with low to medium heat, for 30-40 minutes.

When the chicken pieces are cooked, remove them to a warm dish. Mix the cornflour and water to a paste and stir into the hot juices. Carefully move the pan over to the lit side of the barbecue and simmer gently, stirring continuously, until the sauce has thickened.

Allow your guests to pour the hot sauce over the chicken. Serve with rice and a salad.

PoultryandGame

Streaky drumsticks

Serves 4

8 plump chicken drumsticks
75g (3oz) cream cheese
8 rashers of streaky bacon
groundnut or sunflower oil for basting
salt and freshly ground black pepper

Soak 8 wooden cocktail sticks in water.
Preheat and prepare the barbecue for grilling,
following the instructions on page 8.

Using a short, sharp knife, make a deep
incision in the fattest part of each drumstick
and fill the slit with cream cheese. Season;
then wrap a rasher of bacon around each
drumstick and secure in place with the soaked
wooden cocktail sticks.

Cook, over medium to high heat, basting
frequently with oil, for about 12 minutes each
side or until cooked.

Barbecued pheasant with wine sauce

Pheasant should be hung for at least three
days for a decent flavour to develop, and the
meat to become tender. Hens (with the dull
brown plumage) are plumper and more
succulent than cock birds, and are generally
considered to make better eating.

Serves 2-4

1 plump pheasant, well hung
3 tablespoons soft butter
3 slices streaky bacon
3 tablespoons port or red wine
1 garlic clove, chopped finely
salt and freshly ground black pepper

Prepare the barbecue for 'Indirect heat'
cooking, following the instructions on page 10.
(Use a drip pan.)

Carefully wipe the pheasant inside and out
with a damp cloth. Spread the butter over the
outside of the bird and place the slices of
bacon across the bird's breast. Cover the wing
tips and the knuckle ends of the legs with foil.
Season with salt and pepper.

Cook, with medium heat, for 1-1¼ hours,
removing the bacon during the last 15
minutes of cooking to allow the breast to
brown. To check that the pheasant is cooked,
press the plumpest part of a thigh (protect the
fingers with kitchen paper) - it should feel soft.

Place the pheasant on a warm platter and
leave it to rest for a few minutes before
carving. Lift out the drip pan and stir the port
or red wine and chopped garlic into the juices.
Heat the sauce mixture on the barbecue and
serve with the pheasant.

Spit-roasted glazed duckling

Serves 3-4

1.75-2.25kg (4-5 lb) plump young duckling

Marinade:

4 tablespoons dry red wine

1 teaspoon soy sauce

2 tablespoons sugar

3 tablespoons groundnut oil

1 teaspoon paprika

$^1/_2$ teaspoon freshly grated root ginger or a good pinch of ground ginger

a pinch of ground cinnamon

a pinch of grated nutmeg

a pinch of freshly ground black pepper

2 tablespoons clear honey

Carefully wipe the duckling inside and out with a damp cloth and pat dry with kitchen paper.

Mix together the ingredients (except the honey) for the marinade. Spread the mixture over the inside and outside of the bird and wrap it completely in foil. Place the wrapped duckling in a refrigerator and leave for 24-36 hours. Remove it about two hours before cooking.

Prepare the barbecue for spit roasting, following the instructions on page 12.

Remove the duckling from the foil, reserving any remaining marinade. Run a spit through the exact centre of the bird, firmly set the spit forks in the thighs and breast and test for balance (see page 12).

Position the spit on the barbecue and cook over medium heat if spit roasting with the barbecue lid down, or over medium to high heat if open spit roasting. Cook for about 1$^1/_2$ hours or until the thigh meat is soft when squeezed (protect the fingers with kitchen paper). Baste occasionally with the reserved marinade. Stir the honey into the marinade 15 minutes before the end of cooking and baste the duckling several times with the mixture so the skin is richly glazed.

Carve and serve immediately.

Grilled marinated quail

Unlike pheasant, quail should be eaten really fresh, preferably within twenty-four hours of being killed. This recipe calls for three quail per serving: two quail per head should still be adequate, but one quail per guest only stirs the appetite without satisfying it and brands the host-cook as stingy.

Serves 4

12 quail, drawn and split lengthways through the breastbone

125g (4oz) butter, melted

Marinade:

600ml (1 pint) dry white wine

3 tablespoons lemon juice

1½ tablespoons red or white wine vinegar

3 garlic cloves, crushed

1 teaspoon dried whole tarragon or rosemary leaves

1 teaspoon dried thyme

1 bay leaf

1 teaspoon salt

¼ teaspoon freshly ground black pepper

To make the marinade, mix together the ingredients in a large saucepan and heat until simmering. Remove the pan from the heat, cover and allow to stand for 1-2 hours.

Pour the marinade into a dish and add the quail to the mixture, turning the birds over a few times before covering the dish. Refrigerate for 6-8 hours or overnight.

Prepare the barbecue for grilling, following the instructions on page 8.

Remove the quail from the marinade, drain and then pat dry. (Either discard the marinade or freeze it for future use.)

Grill the quail, cut side down, over medium heat for about 15-20 minutes, turning them occasionally and basting when you do so, with the melted butter.

Serve immediately.

Stir-fried chicken with peppers in a sherry sauce

(pictured on page 87)

Serves 3-4

375g (12oz) chicken breasts, boned and skinned

1 teaspoon salt

2 teaspoon cornflour

2 tablespoons groundnut oil

1 medium-size green pepper, de-seeded and cut into 2.5cm (1 inch) pieces

1 medium-size red pepper, de-seeded and cut into 2.5cm (1 inch) pieces

2 dried red chilli peppers, de-seeded and cut into fine shreds

1 tablespoon lard

Sherry sauce:

3 tablespoons chicken stock

2 tablespoons dry sherry

1¹/₂ tablespoons red wine vinegar or 1 tablespoon Balsamic vinegar

1 tablespoon tomato purée

2 teaspoons cornflour

Slice the chicken into small bite-size cubes. Sprinkle over with the salt and cornflour and rub all together with 2 teaspoons of oil. Combine the sauce ingredients in a bowl, mix well and put to one side.

Prepare the barbecue for wok-cooking, following the instructions on page 14.

Heat the wok on the barbecue and add the remainder of the oil. When the oil is hot, add the chicken and stir-fry for about 2 minutes or until the chicken has nicely browned. Remove the chicken to a bowl and keep warm adjacent to the barbecue. Melt the lard in the wok and add the sweet peppers and prepared sauce. Stir and cook until the sauce starts to boil before returning the chicken. Stir-fry for a further 2 minutes.

Serve immediately.

Spit-roasted saddle or loin of venison

(pictured on page opposite)

Gooseberry or redcurrant jelly make delicious accompaniments to this handsome dish.

Serves 6-8

1.75-2.25kg (4-5 lb) saddle or loin of venison, trimmed of fat

125g (4oz) salt pork, cut into thin strips

2 garlic cloves, each cut into 4 slivers

Basting sauce:

175g (6oz) clear honey

150ml ($^1/_4$ pint) soy sauce

300ml ($^1/_2$ pint) orange juice

juice of 1 lemon, strained

150ml ($^1/_4$ pint) tomato ketchup

300ml ($^1/_2$ pint) red wine vinegar

1 teaspoon salt

$^1/_2$ teaspoon freshly ground black pepper

1 teaspoon mustard powder

$^1/_2$ teaspoon paprika

Prepare the barbecue for spit-roasting, following the instructions on page 12.

Wipe the venison with a damp cloth. Make slits in the meat and lard generously with the salt pork. Push the garlic slivers well down into the slits.

In a small pan mix together the honey, soy sauce, orange and lemon juice, tomato ketchup, wine vinegar, salt, pepper, mustard and paprika over low heat until blended.

Place the roast on the spit, balance it (see page 12) and secure firmly with the spit forks. Brush the venison generously with the basting sauce and cook over medium heat if spit roasting with the barbecue lid down, or over medium to high heat if using an open barbecue, until a meat thermometer inserted into the thickest part reads 60°C/140°F for rare meat or 85°C/185°F for well-done meat.

Allow the meat to stand for 10 minutes before carving.

Pictured opposite:
Spit-roasted saddle or loin of venison
Orange burgundy duckling
Stir-fried chicken with peppers in a sherry sauce

Christmas Turkey

It's Christmas Day in the workhouse
(the oven's choc-a-bloc, and there are hungry
mouths to feed)
AND the snow is a falling hard
'Where can I cook the Christmas bird?'
(the poor cook wailed)
Why out there in the yard!

(poem by kind permission of Hamish)

Cooking Christmas dinner, with all the scrumptious trimmings, for a hungry gaggle of family and friends is quite a challenge - especially so when the poor old cook has to make do with rather limited cooking resources. However, for those families fortunate enough to possess a covered barbecue, a glorious opportunity presents itself to give the oven, the cook, and especially the member of the after dinner washing-up team who has been ear-marked to clean the fat-splattered oven, a well earned rest and reprieve.

Barbecuing the turkey provides several major benefits:

1. valuable oven space is freed for other pressing duties

2. the oven retains its pristine condition

3. the turkey's succulence, taste, handsome appearance and aroma, at least equals, if not transcends, that of most oven cooked birds AND if the turkey is smoke-cooked (a cooking technique which should only be practised in the great outdoors) the resultant golden mahogany 'tan' will further inflame the taste-buds of the waiting flock!

4. neither rain nor snow will hinder your covered barbecue from doing its duty on Christmas Day, although a cold wind whistling around your back yard will result in a slightly extended cooking time

5. the person whose task it is to brave the elements in order to retrieve the turkey, will, instantly, become the valiant hero of the hungry waiting horde

Method:

Prepare the barbecue for 'Indirect heat' cooking, following the instructions on page 10.

Ensure the giblets and neck have been removed from the turkey. Rinse the turkey all over, and inside its neck and body cavities; pat dry with kitchen towelling. Sprinkle the cavities generously with salt and pepper.

Tuck the wings behind the back but leave the legs free ie. not tucked into the band of skin by the parson's nose, or tied closely together.

Use your hand, or a brush, to spread groundnut oil, or softened butter or margarine, all over the bird.

Lightly season the oiled surfaces with salt and freshly ground black pepper.

Position the turkey on the barbecue, partially shielding its lower sides with a narrow band of foil (tucking one edge of the foil under the bird's back will help to secure the foil). Wrap a band of foil 10-12cm (4-5 inches) wide around each knuckle and lower part of the legs.

Cook the turkey, with the lid down, until a meat thermometer registers 185°F/100°C when positioned deep into the inside of the leg (making sure that the tip of the thermometer does not touch the bone-to give a false reading).

The cooking time will vary considerably depending upon fuel type, size of barbecue, weather conditions and of course the weight of the bird, but a 5-6kg (11-13 lb) turkey should take around 2-2^1/$_2$ hours. Allow 20-30 minutes additional cooking time if the bird is fully stuffed at the neck. The stuffing can be baked separately in an ovenproof dish, by placing one or two oven-proof dishes fore and/or aft of the bird (not directly over the fire-bed) during the final 50-60 minutes of cooking.

The Finale:
Having given the waiting guests a brief glance of the golden bird, just to get their juices up and running, let it to rest for 20-25 minutes before carving.

 Roughly halfway through roasting a bird, turn it 180° to avoid uneven cooking.

Hickory smoked turkey with a Scottish glaze

If you want to make your Christmas turkey look even more sensational, even more tasty, cook as above but add 2-4 chunks, or 2-4 handfuls of small chips, of hickory wood (previously soaked in water) to the barbecue's fire-bed roughly halfway through the cooking period. Adding the wood earlier will intensify the bird's colour and piquancy. During the final 15-20 minutes of cooking, brush the bird all over with a glaze made by mixing about 50g (2oz) of butter with 2-3 tablespoons of Drambuie or your favourite single malt or favourite liqueur.

Venison steaks with Cranberry and red wine sauce

Serves 4-6

750g-1kg (1¹/₂-2 lb) loin of venison, boned and tied

salt pork or fat bacon, for larding (optional)

softened butter for basting

1 tablespoon juniper berries, crushed

Marinade:

250ml (8floz) dry red wine

1 medium-sized onion, sliced

1 medium-size carrot, sliced

1 large bouquet garni

2 tablespoons olive oil

1 tablespoon red or white wine vinegar

6-8 black peppercorns

Sauce:

2 tablespoons oil

2 shallots or 1 small onion, chopped finely

1 small carrot, chopped finely

¹/₂ celery stick, chopped

1 tablespoon plain flour

450ml (¹/₄ pint) beef bone stock

1 tablespoon cranberry jelly

Cut the rolled loin into steaks (they will look similar to tournedos) 2.5-4cm (1-1¹/₂ inches) thick. Lard these steaks with salt pork or fat bacon, if desired.

To make the marinade, mix together the ingredients in a pan, bring to the boil and then leave until cold.

Place the steaks in a shallow dish and pour over the cold marinade. Cover the dish and leave for 6-8 hours or overnight in the refrigerator. If refrigerated, remove about 2 hours before cooking.

To prepare the sauce, heat the oil in a pan, add the shallots or onion, carrot and celery and cook until lightly coloured. Stir in the flour and cook slowly until the vegetables are nicely browned. Gradually stir in the stock and cook gently for about 30 minutes. Skim and strain the sauce. Then return it to the pan and continue simmering.

Prepare the barbecue for grilling, following the instructions on page 8.

Remove the steaks from the marinade, reserving the marinade, and dry them with kitchen paper. Strain the marinade into the sauce and let it continue to simmer, skimming any scum from the surface. Add the cranberry jelly and continue simmering until the sauce is syrupy.

Meanwhile, sear the steaks over high heat for about 10 seconds on each side. Move the steaks to the sides of the grill. Reduce the heat to low/medium (if using a gas unit) or move the meat to a cooler spot on a charcoal unit, and continue grilling the steaks, basing frequently with softened butter, for a further 3-4 minutes on each side, adding the crushed juniper berries as you turn them, until cooked to the desired degree.

Spoon a little of the sauce over the venison steaks and serve immediately.

Serve the remaining sauce separately.

Grilled lobster

Fresh lobster is available during the spring/summer months. Females not only make better eating but also provide the coral for making delicious coral butter. This recipe is in the 'unashamed luxury' class.

Serves 2

2 live female lobsters each weighing about 500g (1 lb)

175g (6oz) butter

1 teaspoon paprika

salt and freshly ground black pepper

1 lemon, cut into wedges, to serve

Kill the lobsters by laying them on their backs and inserting the tip of a sharp knife between the body shell and tail segment - thus severing the spinal cord. Otherwise, plunge each lobster head first into vigorously boiling water, using tongs to hold it under the surface for 2-3 minutes (the lobster will begin to turn red).

Prepare the barbecue for grilling, following the instructions on page 8.

Place the lobsters on a cutting board and split length-ways by drawing a sharp knife down the centre of the back. Discard the black intestine running down the middle of the tail and the white gills from the top of the head. Remove the bright red coral or roe and keep to one side.

Mix together 50g (2oz) of the butter, the paprika, and a pinch each of salt and pepper. Spread over the lobster flesh.

Grill the lobsters, cut side down, over medium to medium/high heat, for 5-7 minutes. Turn the lobster halves and cook for 10 minutes or so. (By doing this the lobster's shell will retain most of the meat juices.) The lobster is ready to eat when the tail meat becomes opaque.

Blend the remaining butter with the reserved coral or roe. Serve the lobsters with the coral butter and the lemon wedges.

Griddled Coquille St Jacques with coriander and lime butter

Griddled scallops will make a delicious, if a little pricey, light main course for that special 'barbecue a deux'

Bon appetite.

Serves 2

10 large fresh, or frozen, scallops

(If using fresh, ask your fishmonger to clean them but insist on keeping the shells. They will come in handy as ash trays for your next barbecue party.)

2 tablespoons chopped fresh coriander leaves

50g (2oz) butter, at room temperature

juice of 1 lime

10 large scallops, with their coral intact

Blend the coriander, butter and lime juice together.

Prepare the barbecue for grilling, following the instructions on page 8.

Melt the coriander and lime butter on the barbecue's griddle plate, or in a large heavy-based grill pan. Place the scallops about 5cm (2 inches) apart on the greased surface of the griddle plate, or grill pan, and cook, over a medium to high heat, for 4-5 minutes until firm, occasionally spooning some of the melted herby butter over the scallops. Test regularly over the last 2-3 minutes of cooking as they can easily overcook.

Serving suggestion:

A tomato salad and some very small, very new potatoes.

Sardines asadas with herb and garlic butter

(pictured on page 6)

To impart that little bit of extra oceanic flavour to the cleaned sardines, bury them in coarse salt and leave to cure for 2-3 hours. Brush off most of the salt before proceeding to oil, season and grill the fish. Frozen sardines may be used, but thaw them thoroughly beforehand.

Serves 4

20 small fresh sardines, cleaned

4 tablespoons olive oil, plus extra for greasing

salt and freshly ground black pepper

1 quantity of Herbs and Garlic butter (page 161), to serve

Prepare the barbecue for grilling, following the instructions on page 8.

Pat the fish dry. Brush lightly with the oil and season to taste with salt and pepper. Place the fish on a well-oiled grill and cook, over high heat, for about 3-4 minutes each side.

Serve the sardines with pats of the Herb and Garlic Butter.

Baked whole fish

This recipe is particularly suitable for sea bass, salmon or red mullet.

Serves 6-12

1 whole fish weighing 1.75-3kg (4-7 lb) cleaned and scaled if necessary

4 spring onions, chopped very finely

1 teaspoon salt

1 teaspoon sugar

1 teaspoon freshly grated root ginger

1 tablespoon soy sauce

1 tablespoon sake or dry sherry or dry wine

1 tablespoon groundnut or 2 teaspoons sesame oil, plus extra for brushing

Wipe the fish inside and out with a damp cloth and pat dry with kitchen paper. Remove the fins but leave the head and tail intact unless you object strongly to leaving the head on. Score the fish, almost to the bone, with 3 parallel diagonal slashes, on each side.

Combine the spring onions, salt, sugar, ginger, soy sauce, sake, sherry or wine and chosen oil. Rub the fish inside and out with this mixture. Allow the fish to stand, in a cool place, for 30 minutes.

Prepare the barbecue for 'Indirect heat' cooking, following the instructions on page 10.

If you have a fish broiler large enough to accommodate the fish, brush the inside of the cage with oil before enclosing the fish. Alternatively, make an aluminium pan (see page 168) large enough to take the fish. Brush the inside surface of the pan with oil before adding the fish.

Cook the fish with medium to high heat. If using a fish broiler, allow 10 minutes total cooking time for every 2.5cm (1 inch) of the fish's thickness (at its thickest point). Allow 2-3 minutes extra per 2.5cm (1 inch) if cooking the fish in a foil pan. Brush frequently with oil during cooking and carefully turn the fish halfway through cooking. When the fish is done, the skin will be nicely browned and the flesh easily flaked with a fork. Do not overcook!

FishandShellfish

Fish steaks with sweet and sour sauce

Serves 6

6 fresh or frozen halibut, haddock, cod
or swordfish steaks, 2.5cm (1 inch) thick

oil for greasing

Sweet and sour sauce:

150ml ('/4 pint) dry white wine

2 tablespoons white wine vinegar

2 tablespoons oil

300ml ('/2 pint) crushed pineapple
with juice

1 tablespoon soy sauce

2 teaspoons lemon juice

1/2 teaspoon mustard powder

1/2 teaspoon garlic salt

1 1/2 tablespoons brown sugar

1 tablespoon chopped onion (optional)

Thaw the steaks, if frozen. Arrange the fish
steaks in a shallow dish.

Mix together the ingredients for the sauce.
Pour the sauce over the steaks, cover and
leave in the refrigerator for 30 minutes,
turning once.

Prepare the barbecue for grilling or 'Indirect
heat' cooking, following the instructions on
page 10.

Briefly drain the fish and reserve the sauce.
Place the fish steaks in an oiled wire broiler
(prior to placing on an oiled grill), or on a
greased griddle plate, and cook, over medium
heat, for 5 minutes each side or until the fish
flakes easily with a fork, basting with the
sauce several times during cooking.

Alternatively, arrange the steaks in a shallow
baking tin, baste with the sauce and cook by
the 'Indirect heat' method, allowing an extra
8-10 minutes total cooking time. Turn over the
steaks carefully about halfway through
cooking and baste them with the sauce.

Grilled salmon steaks

Serves 6

4 salmon steaks about 2.5cm (1 inch) thick

1 teaspoon very finely chopped onion

$^1/_2$ teaspoon paprika

a generous pinch of garlic salt

2 teaspoons lemon juice

oil or melted butter for brushing

salt and freshly ground white pepper

Wipe the fish with a damp cloth. Season both sides of the salmon steaks with salt and freshly ground pepper.

Stir the onion, paprika, garlic salt and a little more pepper to taste, into the lemon juice. Brush both sides of the salmon steaks with the marinade and leave in a cool place for about 30 minutes. Drain briefly, reserving any liquid.

Prepare the barbecue for grilling, following the instructions on page 8.

If using a hinged broiler, brush oil over the inside. Place the steaks inside and cook over medium to high heat for 5-6 minutes each side, basting frequently with any leftover marinade. Otherwise, place the steaks directly on to a well oiled grill or greased griddle plate.

Alternatively, tear off four pieces of 46cm (18-inch) heavy-duty foil large enough to 'Drugstore wrap' each steak. Brush melted butter all over the shiny side of each piece of foil. Place a marinaded salmon steak in the centre of the buttered surface. Having spooned a little of the marinade over the fish, bring the two long sides of the foil together above the steak. Fold over twice (leaving some space above the steak to allow for heat circulation and expansion); then fold the short ends in the same way to make a fairly leak-proof package. Place the foil packages on the grill and cook, over medium to high heat, for about 10 minutes each side or until the fish flakes easily.

Serve the hot salmon steaks on a bed of stir-fried vegetables.

Stuffed mountain trout

This recipe has been kindly provided by Graham Ducker, a close friend and colleague in the barbecue industry. Graham, a highly experienced barbecue cook, is a keen devotee of the 'Pit Barbecue' (the steam engine look-a-like reviewed on page 163) and the following recipe is one that he frequently tackles on his 'Cactus Jack' barbecue smoker. Graham reckons that trout is one of 'the premier freshwater fish for barbecuing, which will enjoy a swim in the smoke of a barbecue smoker'. Although his recipe talks of 'mountain trout', he assures me that trout which swim horizontally in lowland rivers, will do just as well. In this preparation the bacon does the work of a fat-baster.

Serves 4

Trout paste:

4 garlic cloves

juice of $^1/_2$ lemon

1 teaspoon Worcester sauce

1 teaspoon fresh ground black pepper

$^1/_2$ teaspoon salt

1 teaspoon vegetable oil

4 boned trout approx. 8oz each

8 slices bacon

6 tablespoons chopped onion

6 tablespoons chopped green pepper

6 tablespoon finely chopped celery

1 packet plain crisps (crushed)

6 tablespoons chopped pecans

About $1^1/_2$ hours before you plan to barbecue, prepare the paste by mashing or chopping the garlic in a pestle and mortar, or mini-food processor. Mix in the lemon juice, Worcester sauce, pepper and salt. Then blend in the oil to make a paste. Rub the trout inside and out with paste. Wrap the trout in food wrap and refrigerate for about 1 hour.

Prepare the 'Pit barbecue' (smoker) for barbecuing, or alternatively, prepare a lidded charcoal or gas barbecue for 'smoke-cooking' (following the 'Indirect heat' cooking technique detailed on page 10). In the former case use well seasoned logs of wood, such as beech, ash, sycamore or fruitwood. In the latter case use chips, or small chunks, of the above hardwoods, or oak, which will be more readily available at your local barbecue emporium. (See page 11 for further advice on smoke cooking.) Whatever the type of barbecue you are using, bring the unit's cooking temperature to a low 80-100°C on the heat indicator.

Remove the trout from the refrigerator and let them sit at room temperature for approximately 20 minutes.

On the barbecue's griddle plate, or in a heavy skillet, fry the bacon over medium heat, removing the bacon whilst it is still limp. Set the bacon aside. Add the onion, pepper and celery to the bacon drippings and saute briefly until softened. Remove the mixture from the heat and stir in the crushed crisps and pecans. Stuff each trout with a portion of this filling. Wrap two slices of the partially cooked bacon around each fish, securing with soaked toothpicks as needed.

Transfer the trout to the smoker, or covered charcoal or gas barbecue, and cook until the bacon is browned and crisp and the fish opaque and easily flaked. This should take 40-50 minutes.

Serve immediately

Graham's tip: *Trout can take a heavier level of smoke induced flavour than most fish, making them particularly suitable for the log-burning Pit barbecues.*

Angels on horseback

Serves 4

8 canned or raw oysters, shelled
1 tablespoon lemon juice
8 thin rashers of bacon
melted butter for brushing
salt and freshly ground black pepper
4 slices of hot, buttered toast, to serve

Soak 8 wooden cocktail sticks in water, if using cocktail sticks.

Prepare the barbecue for grilling, following the instructions on page 8.

Sprinkle the oysters with the lemon juice, salt and pepper. Wrap each oyster in a bacon rasher and fasten with a soaked wooden cocktail stick or a fine metal skewer.

Brush the skewered oysters with melted butter and grill, over medium to medium/high heat, for about 3-4 minutes, turning them several times. Do not overcook.

Serve immediately, with the prepared toast.

Grilled spicy trout with salsa
(pictured on page 107)

Serves 4

4 x 250g (8oz) trout, cleaned

2 tablespoons ground cumin

1 tablespoon ground coriander

juice of $1/2$ lemon

1 tablespoon olive oil

freshly ground black pepper

Salsa

2 tablespoons fresh coriander, chopped

250g (8oz) ripe tomatoes, de-seeded and diced

1 small red onion, very finely chopped

juice of $1/2$ lemon

salt and freshly ground black pepper, to taste

Mix the salsa ingredients together and adjust seasoning to taste. Set aside for the flavours to blend.

Cut 5 diagonal slashes in both sides of each trout. Mix the ground cumin, ground coriander and salt together and rub the mixture all over the trout and well into the slashes. Leave in a cool place for about 20 minutes.

In the meantime prepare the barbecue for grilling, following the instructions given on the page 8.

Season the trout with salt and freshly ground black pepper, drizzle with lemon juice and oil and place on an oiled griddle plate, or grill. Cook, over medium heat, for about 5 minutes on each side (follow the principle of allowing 10 minutes total cooking time, per 2.5cm (1 inch) of the fishes thickness).

Serve the spicy trout with the salsa.

Tickled trout

Tickling trout is no laughing matter for either the fish or fisherman. The trout I tickled and caught as a very young boy, was all of 10cm (4 inches) long (and that is probably stretching things a little!)

Serves 4

4 x 375g (12oz) trout, cleaned and boned

oil for brushing

2 tablespoons melted butter

1 quantity of Maitre d'hotel butter, page 161, softened

Marinade:

3 tablespoons olive oil

1 medium-sized onion, chopped finely

1 teaspoon French mustard

1 tablespoon very finely chopped chives

2 tablespoons very finely chopped dill

1 teaspoon salt

1 teaspoon lemon juice

$^1/_2$ teaspoon freshly ground black pepper

Remove the heads from the trout, if desired. Cut and flatten the fish, and place them flesh-side down in a shallow dish.

Combine the oil, onion, mustard, chives, dill, salt, lemon juice and pepper and mix thoroughly. Pour this marinade over the fish, cover and refrigerate for about an hour, turning the fish once.

Prepare the barbecue for grilling, following the instructions on page 8.

Brush oil over the inner surfaces of the broilers. Alternatively, brush oil over the cooking grill, or griddle plate, just before placing the fish.

Place the fish, flesh side down, into the broilers, or straight on to the grill, and cook over medium heat for about 2 minutes. Turn the fish over and brush the melted butter over the cooked side. Continue grilling for a further 3-4 minutes, or until the skin is crisp and the flesh white and easily flaked. Do not overcook.

Spread the Maitre d'hotel butter over the fish just before serving.

Mackerel parmesan

Serves 4

4 fresh mackerel each weighing about 300g (10oz)

oil for greasing

Marinade:

125ml (4floz) oil

4 tablespoons lemon juice

2 tablespoons chopped fresh parsley

¹/₂ teaspoon dried basil

¹/₂ teaspoon salt

¹/₄ teaspoon freshly ground white pepper (if unavailable, black peppercorns will do)

Coating:

75g (3oz) parmesan cheese, grated

25g (1oz) dry white breadcrumbs

¹/₂ teaspoon garlic salt

Clean and rinse the mackerel thoroughly inside and out under cold running water. Wipe dry with kitchen paper.

Place the fish side by side in a shallow dish.

Mix together the oil, lemon juice, parsley, basil, salt and pepper for the marinade. Pour the marinade over the fish, cover and keep in the refrigerator for 1 hour, turning the fish once or twice.

Prepare the barbecue for grilling, following the instructions on page 8.

Lift the fish from the marinade, drain briefly and reserve the marinade.

In a shallow dish combine the cheese, breadcrumbs and garlic salt. Thickly cover the fish with the cheese mixture, which should be pressed firmly on to the skin. Drizzle over with some of the reserved marinade. Placing the mackerel in oiled broilers will help considerably with their handling. Regardless of whether or not you are utilising fish broilers, the fish should be placed directly onto a well oiled grill or griddle plate and cooked, over medium heat, for about 5 minutes. Turn the fish and cook for a further 5-6 minutes or until the flesh flakes easily when prodded with a fork in the thickest part. Baste the fish frequently with the reserved marinade during cooking.

Grilled red mullet
with fennel

The marvellous flavour of the fish will be enhanced if you leave the liver inside the fish during cooking. Once the fish is cooked the liver can be extracted carefully and then pounded with a tablespoon of chopped capers, a tablespoon of chopped oregano, and 3 to 4 tablespoons of olive oil. This mixture makes a very tasty salad dressing. To further increase the aromatic flavour of the fish, try placing a handful of dried fennel stalks on the hot rocks just before you commence cooking. The scented smoke from the fennel stalks will help to stimulate the appetites of neighbours down wind, and of course your guests!

Serves 4

4 large or 8 small red mullet

Marinade:

1 tablespoon melted butter

2 tablespoons oil

$1/2$ teaspoon black peppercorns, cracked

2 tablespoons dry white or red wine

2 garlic cloves, chopped finely

3 large bay leaves, each broken into 4 pieces

1 tablespoon chopped fresh fennel leaves

Clean the fish, but leave the liver (a delicacy of excellent flavour) intact. Make two deep cuts on each side of each fish. Mix together the ingredients for the marinade and pour over the fish. Marinate for about 1 hour.

Prepare the barbecue for grilling, following the instructions on page 8.

Drain the fish, reserving the marinade, and grill over medium to high heat for 5-8 minutes on each side, depending on the size and thickness of the fish. Baste each side of the fish twice during cooking, with the reserved marinade.

FishandShellfish

Herring grilled with fresh herbs

A very handsome fish that is at its very best in the summer. The dish is delicately flavoured, but beware of the bones. So do keep in mind that profound old Spanish saying, 'Telling lies and eating fish, requires great care!'

Serves 4

4 medium-size fresh herring, cleaned

125g (4oz) butter

$^1/_4$ teaspoon ground cardamom

$^1/_2$ teaspoon ground coriander

$^1/_2$ teaspoon salt

a good pinch of freshly ground black pepper

300ml ($^1/_2$ pint) natural yoghurt

oil for brushing

sprigs of fresh fennel, dill or thyme

Scrape the fish to remove all the scales, discard the heads and trim the tails. Make three diagonal cuts across each side of the body. Pat the fish dry with kitchen paper.

Prepare the barbecue for grilling, following the instructions on page 8.

Melt the butter in a small saucepan and stir in the cardamom, coriander, salt, pepper and yoghurt. Brush the fish generously, inside and out, with the seasoned butter.

Place the fish in well oiled fish broilers. (An oiled rectangular steak or hamburger broiler will suffice, providing it is large enough to accommodate the fish.) Otherwise, place the fish directly on to a well oiled grill or griddle plate.

Cook the fish, over high heat, for 5-6 minutes each side until the skin is crisp and the flesh flakes easily with a fork. Baste the fish frequently with the seasoned butter and occasionally place sprigs of the chosen fresh herb on the fire bed to enhance the fish's aromatic flavour.

Heat any remaining seasoned butter and serve with the fish.

Smoky grilled mussels

Mussels are a very great favourite of mine to such an extent that for me, the words 'moule' and 'drool' are synonymous! I only wish they were readily available all year round rather than only between September and March. However do try out this simple, inexpensive and delicious recipe before standing down your barbecue at summer's end as it might encourage you to repeat the exercise throughout the following winter. Mussels are best eaten on the day of purchase, but if you have to keep them overnight, do so (having washed and scrubbed them) in a bucket full of salted water. Sprinkle some fine oatmeal over the water and leave the bucket in a cool place covered with a damp tea towel.

Serves 4

40-60 mussels

a large bunch of dried herbs, eg. rosemary and thyme

1 quantity of herb and garlic butter or garlic butter (page 161) melted

Place the mussels under running cold water for at least 30 minutes. Scrape away any weed and clean the mussels by scrubbing with a small stiff brush.

Prepare the barbecue for grilling, following the instructions on page 8.

Place the mussels in a single layer on the grill and cook over medium to medium/high heat. Scatter the dried herbs on to the hot rocks throughout the short cooking period (keeping the lid closed will enhance the effect of the scented smoke on the aromatic flavour of the mussels). When the mussels have opened fully, leave them on the grill for another minute. Discard any mussels whose shells have failed to open.

Serve immediately, with your choice of melted herb and garlic or garlic butter.

FishandShellfish

Mussels with herb and garlic stuffing

A golden opportunity to ask the cook to 'show us your mussels'.

Serves 4

40-60 mussels

125g (4oz) butter, at room temperature

1 heaped tablespoon chopped fresh parsley

2 garlic cloves, crushed

1 tablespoon lemon juice

2 tablespoons dry white wine (optional)

salt and freshly ground black pepper

Place the mussels under running cold water for at least 30 minutes. Scrape away any weed and then clean by scrubbing with a small stiff brush.

Prepare the barbecue for grilling, following the instructions on page 8.

Put the prepared mussels into a large, heavy bottomed, pan. Cover the pan with its lid, place the pan on the grill and cook over medium heat until the mussels fully open (it is unnecessary to add liquid at this stage). Remove and discard the empty half shells and any mussels that have failed to open.

Whilst the mussels are cooking, combine the butter, parsley, garlic, lemon juice, wine and salt and pepper in a basin and mix well.

Prepare the barbecue for 'Indirect heat' cooking, following the instructions on page 10. Arrange the mussels, in their half shells, on a baking tray. Spoon a small amount of the butter mixture on to each mussel and cook, with medium to medium/high heat, for about 5 minutes.

Serve immediately, with chunks of fresh bread to mop up the juices.

Grilled oysters with garlic butter

(pictured on page 107)

Before buying your oysters, I strongly recommend that you are in possession of, or can borrow, an oyster knife.

Serves 4

24 oysters

250g (8oz) butter

2 teaspoons very finely chopped garlic

3 tablespoons very finely chopped fresh parsley

juice of 1 lemon

Scrub the oysters well and keep them, flat shell uppermost, covered with a damp cloth in a bucket until ready to cook.

Do not store in water.

Prepare the barbecue for grilling, following the instructions on page 8.

Mix together the butter, garlic, parsley and lemon juice in a saucepan and place so it simmers gently on the grill just before cooking the oysters.

Open the oysters and sever the meat from their shell. Add a teaspoonful or so of the garlic butter to each oyster.

Place the shells in a single layer on the grill and cook over high heat until the juices in the shells are bubbling and the oysters beginning to shrink. (The exact cooking time will depend on personal preference, but overcooking will result in the oysters becoming chewy!)

Serve immediately.

Special baked scallops

Serves 4

25g (1oz) butter, melted

6 large scallops removed from their shells. The shells washed and dried

1 lemon, halved

5 tablespoons double cream

3 tablespoons fresh breadcrumbs

salt and freshly ground black pepper

Prepare the barbecue for 'Indirect heat' cooking following the instructions on page 10.

Put 1 teaspoon of the melted butter in the bottom of 4 of the shells. Quarter the scallops and place 6 pieces in each shell. Season with salt and pepper and add a good squeeze of lemon juice. Spoon over the cream and sprinkle with the breadcrumbs. Dribble the rest of the melted butter over the breadcrumbs.

Bake, with medium to medium/high heat for 8-10 minutes or until the tops are golden brown.

Serve immediately.

Swordfish steaks
à la Niçoise

(pictured opposite)

If swordfish is not available, substitute another firm-fleshed fish such as shark, halibut, turbot or cod.

Serves 4

4 x 250g (8oz) swordfish steaks

oil for brushing

Sauce:

4 tablespoons soft butter

2 tablespoons olive oil

2 garlic cloves, chopped very finely

2 anchovy fillets, soaked, drained and mashed

1 tablespoon finely chopped fresh parsley

3 black olives, stoned and chopped finely (optional)

juice of 1 lemon, strained

freshly ground black pepper

Garnish:

lemon wedges

coarsely chopped fresh parsley

Prepare the barbecue for grilling, following the instructions on page 8.

To make the sauce, melt the butter in a small saucepan. Add the oil, garlic, anchovy fillets, parsley, olives, if using, and lemon juice. Add pepper to taste. Cook over low to medium heat for 10 minutes, stirring occasionally. Keep the pan over very low heat until ready to use.

Brush the swordfish steaks with oil and grill over high heat for 5-10 minutes per side, depending on the thickness of the steaks. Take care not to overcook.

Pour the sauce evenly over the 4 steaks and garnish with lemon wedges and chopped parsley.

Pictured opposite:
Tandoori fish and Stir-fried Szechuan prawns
Swordfish steaks à la Niçoise and Grilled oysters
with garlic butter
Sardines asadas with herb and garlic butter
and Grilled spicy trout with salsa

Jens-Jacob's hinged salmon fillets with piquant sauce

This recipe has been adapted from one kindly provided by an old friend, Jens-Jacob Andersen, a chef/restaurateur in Denmark. J-J informs me that the sauce is known in Denmark as 'Fox sauce'.

Serves 4

1 piece of salmon fillet (with the skin on but the bones removed), 20-30cm (8-12 inches) long, cut from the thick head to middle section of the fish

Salt and freshly ground black pepper

Piquant dill sauce (Fox sauce):

2 tablespoons Dijon mustard

2 tablespoons light brown sugar

1 tablespoon oil

2 tablespoons fresh dill or 2 teaspoons dill weed

$1/2$ teaspoon salt

$1/4$ teaspoon white pepper

Wipe the salmon fillet with a damp cloth. Season with salt and freshly ground black pepper. Cut the fillet crosswise, into four equal pieces. Cut each piece across the centre of its width, down to the skin - taking care not to slice through the skin. Fold the sliced fillet pieces back on themselves, with the skin acting as a hinge.

Prepare the barbecue for grilling, following the instructions on page 8.

To make the sauce, first melt the sugar using about two tablespoons of boiling water. Combine the resultant syrup, in a small bowl, with the rest of the ingredients.

If using a hinged steak/burger broiler (an excellent accessory for this recipe), brush the inside of the broiler well with oil before placing the hinged fillets. Otherwise place the fish directly on to a well oiled grill or griddle plate. Brush the fillets with oil and cook over medium to high heat for 5-7 minutes per side depending upon the thickness of the 'salmon sandwich'. If the hinged fillets prove difficult to cook in an upright position simply cook them on their sides. Take care not to overcook! Serve immediately with a little of the sauce poured over the fish with the remainder of the sauce available for people to help themselves.

Tandoori fish

(pictured on page 107)

Serves 2-3

75g (3oz) butter, melted

$^1/_2$ teaspoon ground nutmeg

1$^1/_2$ teaspoons ground cinnamon

1$^1/_2$ teaspoons ground coriander

juice of 1$^1/_2$ lemons

1 whole white fish weighing around 1kg (2 lb) eg. haddock, cod or any other white, firm-fleshed fish

1 medium-size onion, chopped finely

4 garlic cloves, chopped very finely

2.5cm (1 inch) piece of fresh root ginger, peeled and chopped finely

1 teaspoon ground cumin

$^1/_4$ teaspoon chilli powder

1 teaspoon ground fennel

$^1/_2$ teaspoon paprika

1 teaspoon salt

$^1/_4$ teaspoon freshly ground black pepper

150ml ($^1/_4$ pint) natural yoghurt

First make the basting sauce. Combine the melted butter, nutmeg, $^1/_2$ teaspoon of the cinnamon, $^1/_2$ teaspoon of the coriander and the juice of half a lemon. Blend well and put aside.

Clean the fish; then make three diagonal incisions on each side.

Put the onion, garlic, ginger, cumin, remaining cinnamon and coriander, the chilli, fennel, paprika, salt, pepper and the remaining lemon juice in a food processor (or, preferably, use a pestle and mortar) and blend to make a paste. Stir in the yoghurt. Rub the mixture on the inside and outside of the fish and leave in a cool place for 3-4 hours.

Prepare the barbecue for spit-roasting, following the instructions on page 12, or grilling, following instructions on page 8.

If you prefer to spit-roast the fish, it will be far easier to do so if you are in possession of a spit mounted fish broiler. If you prefer to grill the fish, again, it will be a far easier task if you use a large hinged fish broiler. Brush the inside of the broiler with oil before enclosing the fish. If you do not possess a fish broiler, remember to well oil the grill or griddle plate, of the barbecue immediately prior to placing the fish.

Cook the fish over medium heat, basting frequently with the basting sauce, for 15 minutes if spit roasting or 7-8 minutes per side if grilling bearing in mind the fish grilling formula of allowing a total cooking time of 10 minutes per 2.5cm (1 inch) thickness of fish eg. if the fish is 5cm (2 inches) thick, cook each side for 10 minutes.

Turning a large, partially cooked fish can be a somewhat delicate manoeuvre. I find that using two fish slices, each positioned a third of the way in from the tail and head, helps to keep the fish (and one's 'cool') intact.

FishandShellfish

Maurice's mushroom and scallop kebabs

Serves 2

12 large scallops, removed from their shells. The shells washed and dried

12 mushrooms, closed-cap or large buttons

6 tablespoons melted butter

juice of 1 lemon

salt and freshly ground black pepper

Prepare the barbecue for grilling, following the instructions on page 8.

Place a scallop in each mushroom and push a small bamboo skewer (previously soaked in water) or metal skewer, through their centre to hold them securely in place. Assemble 3 or 6 scallops on each skewer leaving a gap of 2.5cm (1 inch) or so between them. Combine the melted butter and the lemon juice and brush this mixture generously over the kebabs. Lightly season with salt and pepper. Grill over medium heat for about 8 minutes, or until the scallops have just turned opaque and slightly firm to the touch. Do not overcook. Turn and baste the kebabs frequently during cooking with the melted butter.

Pour any remaining butter into a small bowl or jug and serve it with the kebabs.

Stir-fried Szechuan prawns

(pictured on page 107)

Serves 2

500g (1 lb) medium-size raw prawns

2 spring onions, chopped coarsely

2 x 2.5cm (1 inch) pieces of fresh root ginger, peeled and crushed

50g (2oz) mangetout or French beans, cut into 5cm (2 inch) lengths

1/2 teaspoon sesame oil

3 tablespoons rice wine or dry sherry

1 teaspoon sugar

6 tablespoons soy sauce

1 dry red pepper, de-seeded and crushed

2 tablespoons groundnut oil

Pull away the legs from the prawns.

De-vein the prawns by carefully slitting the shell down the back (I find kitchen scissors are best for this task). Try not to dislodge the shell whilst removing the black thread like vein. Rinse the prawns quickly in cold water and pat dry.

Combine all the remaining ingredients, except the vegetable oil, in a dish. Add the prawns to the marinade, cover the dish, and leave in the refrigerator for 2-3 hours, stirring occasionally.

Prepare the barbecue for wok-cooking, following the instructions on page 14. Remove the prawns from the marinade, drain and pat dry with kitchen paper. Reserve the marinade.

Heat the wok on the barbecue and add the oil. When the oil is hot, add the prawns and stir-fry, over high heat, for 3-4 minutes. The prawns are done when they turn a pink colour; take care not to overcook.

Add the reserved marinade to the prawns and bring rapidly to the boil. Serve immediately.

Eric's griddled fish cakes

(pictured on page 112)

This piscatorial riposte to the hamburger recipes displayed earlier in the book, should appeal to those readers who, like me, have fond memories of school-canteen fish cakes. Despite their 'armour-plated' exterior (possibly due to the previous day's batch being re-fried?) they were always very tasty. For this recipe you can use any fish you like, such as haddock, cod, sea bass, red mullet etc, but salmon does give the cakes that little extra richness and élan.

Serves 6 as a main course, 10 as a starter and approximately 24 as an appetiser

425g (14oz) fish, filleted, boned and skinned

300g (10oz) potatoes

3 tablespoons lime juice

2 tablespoons chopped fresh coriander

1 tablespoon chopped fresh basil, optional

1 tablespoon capers, roughly chopped

$^1/_4$ teaspoon cayenne pepper

garlic salt, to taste

3 tablespoons groundnut oil

40g (1$^1/_2$oz) butter

Wash the potatoes, leaving the skins intact. Boil in lightly salted water for 10-12 minutes, for medium-size potatoes, if using small, new potatoes allow 8-10 minutes. Do not overcook. Drain the potatoes and, when cool enough to handle, peel off the skins. Grate the potatoes, using the large holes of the grater, into a good size bowl.

Chop the fish into very small chunks and add to the grated potato along with the lime juice, coriander, basil (if using) and chopped capers. Mix well, but gently (trying not to break up the fish chunks too much) and season with the garlic salt and cayenne pepper.

Take spoonfuls of the mixture and firmly press into the desired cake size.

Prepare the barbecue for grilling, following the instructions on page 8.

If your barbecue incorporates a griddle-plate, allow it to get hot before applying the oil and butter. Otherwise use a heavy-based frying pan placed directly on the barbecue grill. Fry the fish cakes for 3-4 minutes on each side depending upon their size and thickness. You should end up with crusty-golden fish cakes.

Drain on kitchen paper and serve immediately.

Helen Louise's fancy fried rice

Serves 2-3

2 tablespoons vegetable oil

1 medium-size onion, chopped finely

3 streaky-bacon rashers, cut into thin strips

3 eggs

1 teaspoon salt

25g (1oz) butter

375-500g (³/₄-1lb) cooked rice

3 tablespoons peas (fresh or frozen)

3 tablespoons prawns (fresh or frozen), legs removed if fresh, chopped

75-125g (3-4oz) bamboo-shoots, very finely chopped

(fresh asparagus can be substituted if desired)

1 tablespoon soy sauce

Break the eggs into a bowl and beat for about 10 seconds, put the bowl to one side.

Prepare the barbecue for wok-cooking, following the instructions on page 14.

Heat the oil and add the onion and stir-fry for about two minutes until the onion starts to soften. Add the bacon and continue stir-frying for another two minutes or until the bacon has crisped up. Remove the onion and bacon to a dish and keep warm adjacent to the barbecue. Add the butter to the wok. When melted, pour in the beaten egg and leave for about a minute or until just starting to set. At this point add the rice, peas, prawns, bamboo shoots, reserved onion and bacon and the soy sauce. Quickly and thoroughly stir and turn the fried rice mixture, from the bottom up, for 2-3 minutes. If you are using a gas barbecue, turn the heat down to a low setting for these final few minutes.

Serve immediately

Pictured opposite:
Eric's griddled fish cakes
Grilled meat tarts with mushroom and onion filling
Crêpes Julie

Vegetables

Orange and ginger glazed carrots

The orange juice and ginger, combined with the butter or honey, makes an attractive and tasty glaze which combines well with the flavour of carrot. For a more piquant taste, replace the ginger with Worcestershire sauce.

Serves 4-6

1kg (2 lb) new carrots

2 oranges

2 teaspoons freshly grated root ginger or $^1/_2$ teaspoon ground ginger

75g (3oz) butter or 2 tablespoons clear honey

salt

Parboil the carrots in boiling, lightly salted water until barely tender, but still crisp. Drain well. Grate the zest from the oranges. Squeeze out and strain the juice.

Prepare the barbecue for grilling, following the instructions on page 8.

Combine the orange zest, orange juice, ginger, butter or honey in a saucepan and, stirring constantly, bring the mixture to the boil. Simmer gently for about 5 minutes. Dip the carrots in the mixture, coating them completely.

Grill over medium heat for about 5 minutes, regularly turning and basting the carrots with the remaining sauce. If using the honey glaze, turn the carrots more frequently to avoid excessive caramelisation.

Tomatoes Provençale

Serves 4-6

4 tablespoons soft butter

2 tablespoons finely chopped shallots

2 tablespoons chopped fresh parsley

$^1/_2$ teaspoon dried tarragon

a pinch of dried basil

$^1/_2$ teaspoon sugar

3 tablespoons dry white wine

4 medium-size tomatoes, peeled and quartered

2 garlic cloves, chopped very finely

salt and freshly ground black pepper

Prepare the barbecue for grilling, following the instructions on page 8.

Melt 2 tablespoons of the butter in a large skillet, or heavy-based frying pan, over high heat. Add the shallots, parsley, tarragon, basil, sugar and wine. Bring the mixture to the boil, stirring occasionally.

Add the tomatoes and stir gently until they are heated through. Add the remaining butter and the garlic and stir gently until the butter has melted. Remove immediately from the heat, season with salt and pepper and serve.

Sweetcorn with dill

Serves 6

6 young sweetcorn cobs

125g (4oz) butter, softened

1 teaspoon dill weed

6 coriander seeds, crushed

1 teaspoon salt

a pinch of grated nutmeg

Loosen the husks sufficiently to strip away the silk. Soak the cobs in iced water for at least 30 minutes. When ready to cook, drain well.

Prepare the barbecue for grilling, following the instructions on page 8.

Blend together all the remaining ingredients and spread generously over the sweetcorn. Re-position the husks, place each cob on a sheet of aluminium foil and wrap securely. Cook by direct heat, over medium heat, for 15-20 minutes, turning several times.

Bacon-wrapped corn

Serves 6

6 young sweetcorn cobs

1 quantity of garlic butter or Tabasco & lemon butter (page 161), softened

6 rashers of streaky bacon, rinds removed

salt

Remove the corn husks and silk and soak the corn for 30 minutes in lightly salted, iced water. Soak 12 wooden cocktail sticks in water. When ready to cook, drain the cobs well.

Prepare the barbecue for grilling, following the instructions on page 8.

Spread the cobs generously with the selected butter. Wrap a rasher of bacon around the length of each corn and secure with the soaked wooden cocktail sticks. Grill over medium heat for about 25 minutes, turning frequently and basting any uncovered areas of the corn cobs with the softened butter, until the bacon is crisp and the uncovered corn is golden brown.

Vegetables

Pilau rice

This highly spiced rice dish, of Eastern origin, goes well with most meats – particularly when grilled as kebabs.

Serves 4

40g (1¹/₂oz) butter

1 medium-size onion, chopped finely

175g (6oz) long-grain rice, washed and drained

450ml (³/₄ pint) chicken stock or water

a pinch of saffron powder or turmeric

¹/₂ teaspoon dried oregano

salt and freshly ground black pepper

Prepare the barbecue for 'Indirect heat' cooking, following the instructions on page 10.

Melt the butter in an ovenproof baking dish. Add the onion and cook until soft and slightly brown. Add the rice and cook, over moderate heat, for 2-3 minutes.

Stir in the chicken stock or water, saffron powder or turmeric, oregano and salt and pepper to taste.

Cook, with low to medium heat, for 20-25 minutes or until all the liquid has been absorbed and the rice is fluffy and bite-tender.

Cheese and herb stuffed tomatoes

(pictured on page 137)

Serves 4

2 large firm tomatoes

3 tablespoons fresh white breadcrumbs

2 tablespoons finely chopped fresh parsley

1 small garlic clove, crushed

25g (1oz) grated cheese eg. cheddar, mozzarella, etc.

2 tablespoons soft butter

a pinch of dried basil

Prepare the barbecue for grilling, following the instructions on page 8.

Cut the tomatoes in half lengthways and scrape out the seeds using a teaspoon. Combine the remaining ingredients and lightly pack the mixture into the tomato cavities. Place the tomato halves, cut side up, on the grill and cook, over medium heat, for about 10 minutes or until the tomatoes are heated through and the cheese has melted.

Barbecued baked beans

Serves 4-6

125g (4oz) streaky bacon rashers, rinds removed

25g (1oz) butter

1 tablespoon oil

1 large onion, chopped finely

1 celery stick, chopped finely

475g (15oz) can of baked beans in tomato sauce

4 small frankfurter sausages

1 tablespoon horseradish sauce

2 tablespoons Worcestershire sauce

1 teaspoon French mustard

3 tablespoons tomato ketchup

50g (2oz) soft dark brown sugar

Prepare the barbecue for grilling, following the instructions on page 8. Cut the rashers of bacon into pieces about 2.5cm (1 inch) long. Put the bacon into a heavy-based saucepan and heat gently on the barbecue until the fat starts to run. Add the butter, oil, onion and celery and continue to cook gently until the onion is translucent and golden brown.

Put the remaining ingredients into the pan and heat through, stirring frequently. If you wish to give the beans a nice smoky flavour, drop a handful of soaked wood chips, such as hickory, or perhaps some fresh herbs, on to the hot fire bed a few minutes before placing the pan. With the lid down (in between stirring), the aromatic smoke will help to give the beans a nice smoky flavour. Don't worry if the surface becomes a little dry and crusty - this will give a little extra tang to the beans and help evoke images of chuck-wagons of old trundling along the Chisholm Trail.

Potato kebabs Madras

One of my favourite potato dishes. When cooked, the kebabs should have great eye appeal.

Try ringing the changes with the curry to see which flavour/colour you prefer.

Serves 4

750g (1$^1/_2$lb) new potatoes or main-crop potatoes, washed and cut into 2.5-4cm (1-1$^1/_2$ inch) cubes

(Leaving the skin on the potatoes will add to their flavour.)

oil for greasing

6 tablespoons bottled curry paste or curry powder blended with 2-3 tablespoons water

salt

Cook the potato cubes in boiling, salted water until they are barely tender but not overcooked - a fine skewer should push into the potato without undue pressure. Drain thoroughly and, when cool enough to handle, thread the cubes on to oiled (preferably flat-bladed) skewers, leaving a small gap between each cube. Generously brush the cubes with the curry paste or blended curry powder and allow to stand for up to an hour.

Prepare the barbecue for grilling, following the instructions on page 8.

Grill over high heat for about 10 minutes or until the potato cubes are uniformly cooked on all sides Baste the potatoes once or twice during cooking with any leftover paste.

Serve immediately.

117

Vegetables

Roasted potatoes with garlic, rosemary and thyme

(pictured on page 70)

A cracking combination of taste, appearance and aroma. This dish also makes a great appetiser that is far more satisfying than a pinch of crisps, even if the crisps are barbecue flavoured.

Serves 4-6

1kg (2 lb) large new potatoes, washed, leaving skins on, cut into 1cm ('/₂ inch) cubes

2 tablespoons fresh rosemary leaves, finely chopped

1 tablespoon fresh thyme leaves, stripped off the stems

2 garlic cloves, finely chopped

2 tablespoons olive oil

salt and freshly ground black pepper

a shallow steel roasting-tin measuring approximately 30 x 40cm (12 x 16 inches)

Prepare the barbecue for 'Indirect heat' cooking, following the instructions on page 10.

Pour the oil into the roasting-tin and place in the barbecue to heat up.

Thoroughly dry the potato cubes in a clean tea-cloth and transfer onto a tray or large plate. Having carefully pushed the roasting-tin over the barbecue's fire-bed, equally carefully slide the potatoes into the hot oil. Replace the tin in its original position.

Stir the potato around whilst sprinkling over with the rosemary, thyme and garlic.

Continue cooking, with high heat, for 30-40 minutes or until the potatoes are golden brown.

Season with salt and pepper and serve immediately.

Gratin dauphinoise

(pictured on page 121)

The vegetable equivalent of creamy rice pudding?

Serves 4-6

1kg (2 lb) potatoes, preferably Desiree or Edwards or similar

1 large garlic clove, halved, plus 1 small garlic clove, chopped very finely

25g (1oz) butter

1 egg

250ml (8floz) hot milk

250ml (8floz) double cream

50g (2oz) gruyere cheese, grated

freshly grated nutmeg

salt and freshly ground black pepper

Prepare the barbecue for 'Indirect heat' cooking, following the instructions on page 10.

Peel the potatoes and slice them very thinly (a mandoline is perfect for this task). Plunge the potato slices into a bowl of cold water and stir around to wash off some of the starch. Drain and dry the slices very thoroughly in a clean tea-cloth.

Rub the inside of an earthenware gratin dish with the cut garlic and then grease with the butter. Place the potato slices in layers, sprinkling each layer with the finely chopped garlic and nutmeg, salt and pepper to taste.

Whisk the egg, milk and cream together, and pour the mixture over the potato slices, ensuring the top layer is completely covered. Cover the top with the grated cheese.

Cook, with medium heat, for 1-1¼ hours or until the potatoes are tender when pierced with a skewer.

Baked potatoes with toppings

Select nicely shaped, even-size baking potatoes. The ingredients for the toppings need to be well mixed before they are added to the potatoes.

Serves 4

4 medium/large baking potatoes

groundnut or sesame oil

salt and freshly ground black pepper or your choice of barbecue spice

Prepare the barbecue for grilling or 'Indirect heat' cooking, following the instructions on page 8 or 10. Scrub the potatoes well, pat dry and prick deeply all over with a skewer or fork. Brush with oil. (I find it easier, when tackling several potatoes, to use my hands.) Season with salt and pepper or sprinkle generously with barbecue spice. Wrap the potatoes in foil or, if you like a crispy skin, leave the potatoes unwrapped.

Cook by direct heat, over medium to high heat, and turn the potatoes several times during cooking (a medium-size potato will take 45-60 minutes and a large one 60-70 minutes). Alternatively, bake the potatoes by the 'Indirect heat' method, perhaps alongside a joint of meat that you are cooking. This will however take longer and it is a good idea to turn the potatoes over roughly half-way through cooking to avoid the top of the potato turning into 'parchment'.

Cut a cross in the top of each potato and pinch to open out the centre. Top with any of the few suggested toppings or, better still, one of your own creation.

Poor man's caviar with soured cream

4 teaspoons black or red lumpfish roe

150ml (¼ pint) soured cream

1 tablespoon chopped fresh chives

a small pinch of cayenne pepper

Cream cheese and crispy bacon

125g (4oz) cream cheese or grated cheddar cheese

175g (6oz) crisply grilled back bacon, crumbled

50g (2oz) butter

2 tablespoons finely chopped fresh chives

2 teaspoons finely chopped red pepper, to garnish

Avocado and cheese

1 ripe medium-size avocado, chopped roughly

125g (4oz) cream cheese

freshly ground black pepper

Vegetables

Ratatouille

(pictured on page opposite)

I am still unsure whether I prefer ratatouille hot or cold, but one thing is for sure, it certainly goes down well at any temperature with chicken, lamb, beef or fish – or just by itself.

Serves 4-6

1 medium-size aubergine

2 medium-large onions

4 small courgettes

1 medium-size red pepper, de-seeded

1 medium-size green pepper, de-seeded

2 large tomatoes

6 tablespoons olive oil

3 garlic cloves, crushed

1 tablespoon chopped fresh basil or 1 teaspoon dried basil

1 teaspoon dried rosemary

1 bay leaf

1 teaspoon salt

$\frac{1}{2}$ teaspoon freshly ground black pepper

2 tablespoons chopped fresh parsley

Prepare the barbecue for grilling, following the instructions on page 8.

Thinly slice the aubergine, onions and courgettes. Chop the red and green peppers. Remove the skins and seeds from the tomatoes and cut the flesh into wedges.

Place a large skillet on the grill and heat the oil over high heat. Alternatively, if your barbecue can accommodate a baking dish, as per the gas barbecue shown on the opposite page, heat the oil in this. Add the onions and garlic and cook for about 5 minutes or until the onion is soft and translucent. Next add the aubergine, peppers and courgettes. Cook for another 5 minutes, shaking the skillet or stirring the contents of the baking dish frequently.

Add the tomatoes, basil, rosemary, bay leaf, salt and pepper. Sprinkle over the parsley. Bring the lid of the barbecue down, reduce the heat to medium (if using a gas barbecue) and continue cooking for a further 50-60 minutes. Serve the ratatouille hot or cold as a main dish or with chicken, lamb, fish or beef.

Pictured opposite:
Roast chicken with 'Puts'
Ratatouille
Gratin dauphinoise

Crêpes Julie

(pictured on page 112)

A tasty little dish!

50g (2oz) flour

$1/4$ teaspoon salt

1 large egg, lightly beaten

3 tablespoons milk

2 tablespoons single cream

$1/2$ oz butter, melted

225g (8oz) floury potatoes

olive oil, for greasing

25g (2oz) butter

freshly ground black pepper

Sift the flour and the salt into a bowl. Make a well in the centre and pour in the beaten egg.

Using a wooden spoon, beat the mixture, gradually incorporating the milk and cream to make a smooth batter. Finally beat in the melted butter. Cover the bowl and leave for 30-40 minutes.

Meanwhile thinly peel the potatoes and, using the large holes on a grater, grate the potatoes on to 3 layers of kitchen towels. Firmly pat the grated potato with a clean tea-cloth to remove as much of the juice as possible. Add the dried potato to the prepared batter, stir and season generously with freshly ground pepper.

Prepare the barbecue for grilling, following the instructions on page 8.

Lightly grease the barbecue's griddle plate or a large heavy-based frying pan. Add half the butter to melt.

Using 2 tablespoons of potato batter mixture for each crêpe, spoon 4 crêpes into the pan, keeping as much space between them as possible. Spread the batter in thin circles. If you are using a griddle plate, and there is sufficient room to accommodate 8 crêpes, add all the butter prior to cooking.

Cook the crêpes over medium heat for about 5 minutes, or until the undersides are golden. Turn with a spatula and cook for a further 5 minutes or until crisp, golden and cooked through.

Serve immediately.

Herb and sesame new potatoes

(pictured on page 126)

Serves 4-6

1kg (2 lb) new potatoes

50g (2oz) butter

1 tablespoon chopped fresh parsley

1 tablespoon chopped fresh mint

1 tablespoon sesame seeds, toasted

salt and freshly ground black pepper

Peel a 2.5cm (1 inch) strip from the circumference of each potato.

Prepare the barbecue for grilling or 'Indirect heat' cooking, following the instructions on page 8 or 10.

Grease a large piece of heavy-duty aluminium foil (or two layers of ordinary foil) with about half the butter. Place the potatoes together in the centre of the foil and season with salt and pepper. Sprinkle over some of the herbs. Wrap the foil securely around the potatoes, following one of the methods outlined on page 15.

Cook for 40-55 minutes, depending on the size of the potatoes and the cooking technique employed. Check that they are cooked by piercing the top of the foil pack and into the potatoes with a fine metal skewer. Empty the potatoes into a warmed serving dish, sprinkle over with the remaining herbs and sesame seeds and dot with the remaining butter.

Roasted red peppers

Serves 4   (pictured on page 137)

4 large sweet red peppers, de-seeded and cut in half through the stalk leaving the stalk intact

4 medium to large tomatoes

8 anchovy fillets, drained and each chopped into 4 pieces

2 large garlic cloves, finely sliced

3floz (90ml) extra virgin olive oil

freshly ground black pepper

Prepare the barbecue for 'Indirect heat' cooking, following the instructions on page 10.

Lay the pepper halves, cut side up, in an oiled roasting tray. Place the tomatoes in a bowl and pour boiling water over them. After a minute or so, having drained away the water, it should be quite easy to remove the skins from the tomatoes (use a cloth or doubled kitchen paper to protect your hands). Cut the tomatoes into quarters and place 2 quarters in each half pepper to be joined by 4 pieces of the anchovy plus some of the garlic. Dribble two teaspoons of oil over each pepper and season to taste with freshly ground black pepper.

Position the tray on the barbecue and cook, at medium to high heat, for 45 minutes to one hour until the peppers have browned around their edges.

Transfer the cooked peppers to a shallow serving dish and pour over all the juices from the tray.

If serving the roasted peppers as an appetiser, offer your guests a basket of fresh bread chunks to dunk in the delicious juices. Focaccia bread happens to be my favourite 'blotting paper' for this exercise.

123

Vegetables

Spicy nut roast

A delicious recipe that, although produced with the vegetarian in mind, will appeal equally to the taste of many members of the barbecuing carnivora. When cold, it goes well with a salad.

Serves 4

1 tablespoon oil, plus extra for greasing

2 medium-size onions, chopped finely

1 large or 2 small green peppers, de-seeded and chopped finely

50g (2oz) pecan nuts, chopped finely

175g (6oz) walnut halves, chopped finely

75g (3oz) fresh breadcrumbs, preferably wholemeal

1 teaspoon each, chopped fresh thyme and chopped fresh parsley, or
1 teaspoon dried mixed herbs

1 garlic clove, chopped very finely

1 tablespoon mild curry powder or
1 teaspoon hot curry powder

250g (8oz) firm ripe tomatoes, skinned and chopped

1 egg, beaten

salt and freshly ground black pepper

Prepare the barbecue for 'Indirect heat' cooking, following the instructions on page 10.

Heat the oil, add the onions and peppers and gently fry for about 10 minutes, or until they are soft.

Meanwhile, combine the nuts and breadcrumbs together in a large bowl. Add the herbs, garlic, curry powder and seasoning. Stir the onion and pepper mixture, chopped tomatoes and beaten egg into the nut mixture. Bind all together.

Spoon the mixture into a greased 18cm (7 inch) square cake tin, or the equivalent in an ovenproof dish.

Bake, with medium heat, for 30-45 minutes until golden brown.

Mixed vegetable kebabs

You may prefer to concentrate on one vegetable per skewer although, by so doing, the small interchange of flavours created by different vegetables nestling cheek by jowl will be lost.

Serves 6

6 very small potatoes, preferably new
6 small onions or shallots
12 small closed-cap mushrooms
1 large green pepper, de-seeded
2 small courgettes
oil for greasing
50g (2oz) butter, melted
$^{1}/_{2}$ teaspoon garlic salt
$^{1}/_{4}$ teaspoon freshly ground black pepper
6 very small, firm tomatoes
salt

Prepare the barbecue for grilling, following the instructions on page 8. Cook the potatoes and onions separately in lightly salted, boiling water until they are barely tender.

Discard the stems from the mushrooms and wipe the caps. Cut the pepper into 6 pieces. Cut the courgettes into 6 pieces 2.5-4cm (1-1$^{1}/_{2}$ inches) long. Drain the onions and potatoes, and thread all but the tomatoes alternately on to oiled (preferably flat-bladed or twin-pronged) skewers.

Blend together the melted butter, garlic salt and pepper and brush the kebabs generously with the mixture.

Cook, turning frequently and basting with the butter, over medium to high heat, for about 5 minutes. Add a tomato to each skewer and continue cooking, turning and basting, for a further 5 minutes.

Gem squash McTaggart

(pictured on page 127)

Judy McTaggart, an old family friend, fell in love with this exotic vegetable during a photographic safari to Africa. A first-class cook, both indoors and outdoors, this is Judy's recipe for a vegetable which is readily available in supermarkets and greengrocers.

Serves 1-2

1 gem squash
50g (2oz) butter
salt and freshly ground black pepper

Prepare the barbecue for grilling or 'Indirect heat' cooking, following the instructions on page 8 or 10.

Remove the stem, and then cut the squash in half crossways and scoop out the seeds. Place half the butter in each half. Season lightly with salt and a generous amount of pepper.

Place each half in the centre of a square of heavy-duty foil roughly three times the diameter of the vegetable. Bring the four corners of the foil together into a pyramid shape. Loosely fold over the foil edges, where they meet, to seal. Keep the package upright and grill, over high heat, for about 15 minutes; or bake - using the 'Indirect heat' method - for 25-30 minutes.

Most fruit can be cooked directly on the grill over a moderate heat but needs frequent basting with butter or a made-up basting sauce. The alternative, apart from incorporating the fruit in a pie or crumble, is to wrap the prepared fruit, together with the basting juices, in a foil parcel.

Spiced peaches

(pictured opposite)

Spiced peaches are delicious served as a dessert with cream or yoghurt but they also go well with ham, pork and poultry.

Serves 4

5 ripe, firm peaches
50g (2oz) soft brown sugar
1 tablespoon Worcestershire sauce
a pinch of ground cinnamon
a pinch of ground ginger

Halve and stone the peaches.

Place the sugar, Worcestershire sauce, cinnamon and ginger in a saucepan and heat very gently until the sugar has dissolved. Arrange the peach halves in a shallow foil tray and spoon the sugar mixture over them. Leave the peaches for 2-3 hours, turning them occasionally.

Prepare the barbecue for grilling, following the instructions on page 8.

Lightly drain the peaches and grill, over medium heat, until they are just heated through and beginning to brown.

Pictured opposite:
Gem squash McTaggart
Herb and sesame new potatoes

Mixed fruit kebabs
Spiced peaches
Gateau paysanne

Barbados oranges

As an alternative to rum, the equivalent amount of Kirsch liqueur would do very nicely.

Serves 1

1 ripe orange, preferably seedless
1 tablespoon brown sugar
a pinch of ground cinnamon
1 tablespoon rum
1 tablespoon soft butter or margarine

Prepare the barbecue for grilling, following the instructions on page 8.

Peel the orange, removing the pips if necessary, and carefully separate into segments. Place the segments on a piece of doubled aluminium foil. Sprinkle over the brown sugar, cinnamon and rum. Dot the segments with the butter or margarine before wrapping the edges of the foil together securely.

Place the package on the grill and cook, over medium heat, for 15-20 minutes.

Serve topped with whipped cream or vanilla ice cream.

FruitsandPuddings

Mixed fruit and bread kebabs

(pictured on page 126)

A beautiful and colourful composition that is particularly appropriate for 'special' barbecue parties. Take my tip and make up an extra skewer or three which consist solely of bread cubes – as you will discover, they are exceedingly 'moreish' (extra butter and caster sugar will be required if you do so).

Serves 6

2 ripe, firm pears, peeled and cored

melon balls from 1 small melon

juice of 2 lemons

2 oranges, cut into 1cm (^{1}/$_2$ inch) slices

1 small pineapple, peeled and cored, or a 250g (8oz) can of pineapple chunks

12 large, firm strawberries

2 medium, firm bananas, each cut into 3

6 large, seedless grapes

125g (4oz) caster sugar, plus extra for dusting

3 tablespoons of your favourite liqueur

4 tablespoons white wine

1 white loaf, crusts removed

125g (4oz) butter

melted oil for greasing

Cut the pears into large chunks. Place them, together with the melon balls and the lemon juice, in a large bowl. Quarter each orange slice and cut the fresh pineapple, if using, into 2.5cm (1 inch) cubes.

Place the orange pieces, fresh or canned pineapple chunks, strawberries, bananas and grapes in the bowl and add half the sugar, the chosen liqueur and the white wine. Mix gently with your hands and leave the fruit to macerate in a cool place for 20-30 minutes.

Preheat and prepare the barbecue for grilling, following the instructions on page 8.

Slice the bread into 2.5cm (1 inch) cubes and brush each, all over, with the melted butter. Toss the bread cubes in a bowl with the remaining sugar and coat them evenly.

Thread a selection of the fruit, together with two pieces of bread, on to long, oiled metal, preferably flat-bladed, skewers.

Grill over medium heat for about 5 minutes, turning and dusting with more sugar, until the kebabs are lightly caramelised.

If liked, warm the remaining marinade and sprinkle it over the kebabs before serving.

Pam and Ron's famous stuffed pears

This recipe, one of my all time favourites, was borrowed from Pam and Ron Heath, great friends whose culinary skills I have long envied, admired and often sampled.

Serves 6

6 ripe, firm Comice pears, stalks intact
juice of 2 lemons
butter for greasing
caster sugar for dusting
Almond stuffing:
50g (2oz) unsalted butter
25g (1oz) caster sugar
25g (1oz) ground almonds
grated zest of 1 lemon
25g (1oz) glace cherries, chopped finely
a pinch of ground cinnamon
a pinch of ground ginger
1 teaspoon Kirsch (must have)

For the stuffing, cream together the butter and sugar. Add the ground almonds, grated lemon zest, glace cherries, cinnamon, ginger and Kirsch and mix well.

Lightly trim the base of the pears so they can stand upright. Thinly peel the pears, taking care to leave the stalks intact. Put the lemon juice in a saucer. Stand each pear in the saucer and brush liberally all over with the juice. Cut the top off each pear about 2.5cm (1 inch) below the base of the stalk and reserve. Scoop out the pear cores, using a narrow sharp-pointed teaspoon, leaving about 1cm ($^1/_2$ inch) of the flesh at the base intact. Take care not to break through the base of the pear.

Prepare the barbecue for grilling or 'Indirect heat' cooking, following the instructions on page 8 or 10.

Stuff the pear cavities with equal portions of the butter mixture. Replace the pear tops and stand each pear on a lightly greased 25cm (10 inch) square of heavy-duty aluminium foil. Brush the remaining lemon juice over the pears and dust with caster sugar. Gather and twist the foil around the base of the stalks to secure.

Stand the packaged pears in a shallow baking tin or a double thickness foil drip pan (see page 168 on how to make). Cook with medium heat by the 'Indirect heat' method for about 45 minutes, or for about 30-35 minutes by direct heat. The pears are ready when they feel soft when gently squeezed - take care not to overcook them. Handle the pears by the stalks with a gloved hand.

The pears are at their luscious best having been given a few minutes to cool down a little.

Serve the pears with cream, single, double or clotted, or vanilla ice-cream.

129

FruitsandPuddings

Aunt Julia's apple slices

Serves 4

2 large apples, peeled, cored and cut into 2cm (³/₄ inch) thick slices

2 tablespoons lemon juice

40g (1¹/₂oz) butter, melted

2 tablespoons white or brown sugar

1 tablespoon ground cinnamon

1 teaspoon ground ginger (optional)

Spread the slices over a large plate, sprinkle with lemon juice and set aside for a few minutes. Drain off any liquid. Mix together the sugar and cinnamon (and ground ginger if using).

In the meantime Prepare the barbecue for grilling, following the instructions on page 8.

Brush some of the melted butter over the barbecue's griddle plate, or a large piece of doubled aluminium foil set on top of the food grill, and place the slices in a single layer. Brush the slices with the melted butter and lightly sprinkle with roughly half of the sugar mixture. Cook, over medium to high heat, for 3-4 minutes. After turning the slices over, brush with the remaining butter, sprinkle lightly with the sugar mixture and cook for another 3-4 minutes, or until the slices are tender.

Serve immediately, allowing guests, if they wish, to sprinkle more of the sugar/cinnamon mixture over their helping.

Grilled grapefruit

(pictured on page 126)

A refreshing starter, entrée or dessert.

Serves 6

3 grapefruit

3 tablespoons clear honey or brown sugar

3 tablespoons sweet sherry (optional)

6 maraschino cherries

Prepare the barbecue for grilling or 'Indirect heat' cooking, following the instructions on page 8 or 10.

Slice each grapefruit in half, cut the segments loose and remove the pips.

Place each grapefruit half on a piece of doubled aluminium foil large enough to enclose the fruit. Spoon over about half a tablespoon of the honey or brown sugar, and half a tablespoon of the sherry, if using. Put a cherry in the centre of each half before wrapping the edges of the foil together securely.

Place the packages on the grill and cook, over medium heat, for approximately 15 minutes.

Alternatively, omit the cherries, leave the packages open, with the edges turned up to contain the juices, and cook by the 'Indirect heat' method for 15-20 minutes. (By this method, the sugar or honey on top of the grapefruit caramelises.)

Place the cherries on top when the cooking is completed.

Cinnamon stuffed apples

If you are not too keen on cinnamon, try substituting 2 tablespoons of rum (or a little rum flavouring if the stuffed apples are for children's consumption).

Serves 6

6 medium-size cooking apples, cored
125g (4oz) brown sugar
2 teaspoons ground cinnamon
a pinch of ground cloves
40g (1¹/₂oz) walnuts, chopped finely
40g (1¹/₂oz) raisins, chopped finely
1 tablespoon lemon juice
6 teaspoons soft butter

Prepare the barbecue for grilling, following the instructions on page 8.

Place each apple on a piece of doubled aluminium foil about 20cm (8 inches) square. Combine the brown sugar, cinnamon, cloves, walnuts, raisins and lemon juice and use to fill the centres of the apples. Top each apple with a teaspoon of the butter. Bring the edges of the foil up to enclose the apples securely.

Grill the wrapped apples over medium heat for 40-50 minutes, or until the apples feel soft when pressed.

Serve topped with whipped cream or ice cream.

Martin's boozy pineapple

My old pal Martin Cobban is the complete barbecue buff and a leading member of the 'British Barbecue Brigade'. This, apparently, is his favourite barbecue recipe. I wonder why?

Serves 4-6

1 ripe pineapple
2 liquor glasses Kirschwasser (kirsch)
200ml (7floz) carton, crème fraiche

Slice the top 2.5cm (1 inch) off the pineapple, put to one side.

Using a tablespoon, scoop out and reserve, about 4cm (1¹/₂ inches) of pineapple flesh.

Pour 1 glass of the liquor into the cavity. Having drunk the remaining glass, replace the pineapple's top.

Prepare the barbecue for 'Indirect heat' cooking, following the instructions on page 10.

Place the booze-laden pineapple on the barbecue and cook, at a medium heat, for about 35 minutes.

Discarding the 'lid', cut the pineapple into 1cm (¹/₂ inch) slices and serve with the reserved pineapple flesh and a spoonful of crème fraiche.

Rum chocolate banana split

A dish requiring a steady hand, time to spare and sweet-toothed guests in the 2 – 92 age group.

Serves 1 (just about)

1 large, medium-ripe, firm banana

1 teaspoon lemon juice

1 teaspoon rum or a few drops of rum flavouring

25g (1oz) good quality dark eating chocolate, chopped roughly

2 marshmallows, each cut into 8

Peel the banana and place on the centre of a piece of heavy-duty foil (or use a double thickness of ordinary foil) about 23 x 15cm (9 x 6 inches) in size. Sprinkle the lemon juice over the banana to drain down on to the foil.

Using a small-bladed knife, carefully cut a V-shaped wedge from the banana along its length. Reserve the wedge to one side. The cavity should be roughly 1cm ('/2 inch) wide and 1cm ('/2 inch) deep.

Sprinkle the rum or rum flavouring into the cavity. Partially fill the cavity with the chocolate and top with the marshmallow pieces. Press the banana wedge firmly back into place. Lap the long edges of the foil together, leaving a small air space. Firmly squeeze the open ends of the package and turn the crushed ends upwards so the package is roughly gondola-shaped. Chill the package in the refrigerator until required, keeping the 'boat' upright.

Prepare the barbecue for grilling, following the instructions on page 8.

Place the package on the grill and cook over medium heat for about 10 minutes or until the chocolate softens. If cooking lots of bananas, check the progress of one of the packages situated on or near the barbecue's 'hot spot' (see page 181) after 5 or 6 minutes. Overcooking will make the flesh of the banana pulpy and perhaps result in the banana subsiding into an unattractive splodge.

Serve the banana with whipped cream or vanilla ice cream. For the children, shake over some chocolate vermicelli.

Barbecued bread
and butter pudding

I am an associate member of 'BBABPA' (British Bread and Butter Pudding Association) whose prime aim is to promote this quintessential British pud to the world at large. Roast Beef and Yorkshire pudding, along with Cheddar cheese, our superb strawberries and apples (to mention but a few), are recognised, and rightly revered, by foreign gastronomes visiting our shores, but most return home woefully unaware of the above delicacy. Fortunately there are many oases in Great Britain where 'B & BP' appears on the menu and I was fortunate enough to recently consume a truly outstanding example of Brian Turner's renowned Bread and Butter Pudding at his restaurant, 'Turner's', in central London. The following 'naughty but nice' version is probably not one for the 'calorie counters'.

Serves 4

Butter for spreading and greasing

8 thin slices of bread cut from a small loaf

15g ($^1/_2$oz) candied lemon or orange peel, chopped finely

75g (3oz) currants

300ml ($^1/_2$ pint) milk

75ml (3floz) thick double cream

50g (2oz) caster sugar

$^1/_4$ teaspoon grated lemon zest

3 eggs, beaten

a little freshly grated nutmeg

Butter the bread. Grease a 1 litre ($1^3/_4$ pint) oblong baking dish.

Arrange one layer of bread, butter-side-down over the base of the dish. Sprinkle the candied peel and half the currants over the bread and cover with another layer of bread, butter-side-up and the remaining currants.

Combine the milk and cream and stir in the sugar and lemon zest. Whisk the beaten eggs into the mixture and pour over the bread. Sprinkle over a little nutmeg and leave to stand for 30-50 minutes.

Prepare the barbecue for 'Indirect heat' cooking, following the instructions on page 10.

Position the dish on the barbecue and bake, over medium to high heat, for 30-40 minutes or until the pudding is set and the top golden and crisp.

Let the pudding rest for about 10 minutes before eating.

Gateau paysanne

(pictured on page 126)

This traditional French pudding originates from the Normandy department. Based on dessert apples, it is a batter pudding, rather like a clafoutis. It is best served just warm and needs no last minute attention. I have cooked it on numerous occasions at my barbecue cookery demonstrations where it has proved immensely popular with stand staff and visitors alike. Like the wonderful Bread and Butter pudding (page 133) this is one of those puddings that has everyone scrapping to scrape off the crusty little bits left over in the pie dish.

Serves 6-8

750g (1½lb) dessert apples, peeled, cored, quartered and thinly sliced

175g (6oz) caster sugar

2 eggs

200ml (7floz) crème fraiche (this ingredient gives the pud *je ne sais quoi*)

50g (2oz) plain flour

50g (2oz) currants

75g (3oz) butter, plus extra for greasing

optional garnish: **caster or icing sugar**

You will require an ovenproof dish measuring about 20cm x 20cm x 5cm deep (8 inches x 8 inches x 2 inches) or one holding approximately 1.5l (3 pints).

Grease the dish. In a bowl, whisk the sugar with the eggs, then blend in the crème fraiche and the flour to make a smooth batter. Spoon about a third of this batter into a cup (or the empty crème fraiche container) and reserve. Mix the apple slices and currants with the larger quantity of batter. Pour the mixture into the buttered dish and roughly level with the back of a spoon. Try to leave several apple pieces sticking up to burn or caramelise as this will enhance the appearance of the dish.

Prepare the barbecue for 'Indirect heat' cooking, following the instructions on page 10.

Place the dish on the barbecue and bake for about 15 minutes. Allow an extra few minutes if the air temperature is low. Meanwhile, having melted the butter, mix it thoroughly with the reserved batter. Pour the butter/batter mix over the apple/batter mixture and return the dish to the barbecue for a further 15-20 minutes, or until the top of the pudding is golden brown. Remove from the barbecue and allow to cool for several minutes.

Serve with single cream, clotted cream or vanilla ice-cream.

Individual chocolate puddings with a hot chocolate sauce

Serves 4

125g (4oz) self-raising flour

1 rounded tablespoon cocoa powder

$1/2$ teaspoon baking powder

$1/4$ teaspoon bicarbonate of soda

50g (2oz) caster sugar

1 large egg, beaten

1 tablespoon golden syrup

100ml (3$1/2$floz) milk

100ml (3$1/2$floz) sunflower oil

2-3 drops vanilla essence

butter for greasing

Chocolate sauce:

75g (3oz) good quality dark chocolate or 4 tablespoons cocoa butter

25g (1oz) unsalted butter

200ml (7floz) double cream

225g (8oz) icing sugar

Grease 4 x 175ml (6floz) pudding moulds.

Prepare the barbecue for 'Indirect heat' cooking, following the instructions on page 10.

Sift the flour, cocoa powder, baking powder, bicarbonate of soda and caster sugar into a mixing bowl. Pour in the beaten egg together with the golden syrup, milk and oil. Beat to make a smooth batter.

Pour the mixture into the buttered moulds. Having positioned the moulds on a flat metal tray (a sponge tin is fine), place the tray on the barbecue. If using a gas barbecue, adjust the heat control knob to a position between low and medium (a lid-mounted thermometer should show 150°C/300°F). Bake for about 30 minutes, until the puddings feel springy to the touch. If using a charcoal burning unit, make a moderate heat fire-bed and bake for about 30 minutes or until the puddings feel springy to the touch.

To make the sauce, use a double boiler to melt the chocolate (or cocoa butter), unsalted butter and cream together. Gradually add the icing sugar and beat until the mixture becomes glossy. Un-mould onto warmed dessert plates. Pour the chocolate sauce over the puddings and serve.

For a little extra richness, serve with custard or single cream.

Apple pie

(pictured on opposite page)

It seems a long time ago, but I can happily confirm that the pie shown opposite, tasted as just as scrumptious as it looks!

Serves about 6

Shortcrust pastry
As per your usual recipe or as follows:

250g (8oz) plain flour, plus extra for rolling

a pinch of salt

125g (4oz) butter or margarine, cut into small pieces

2-3 tablespoons cold water

milk for brushing

caster sugar for sprinkling

Filling:

500g (1 lb) cooking apples and/or Cox's Orange Pippin dessert apples, peeled, cored and sliced thinly

125g (4oz) brown or white sugar

grated zest of $\frac{1}{2}$ lemon

1-2 cloves (optional)

To make the pastry, sift the flour and salt into a large mixing bowl, add the butter or margarine and rub in until the mixture resembles fine breadcrumbs. Mix in enough cold water with a round-bladed or palette knife to make a stiff dough. Lightly press the pastry into a ball and leave, wrapped in foil or polythene, in the refrigerator for 30 minutes.

Roll out a little more than half the pastry to a circle about 25cm (10 inches) in diameter. Carefully lift the dough to line a 20cm (8 inches) pie dish.

Pile the sliced apples on top and sprinkle over the sugar, lemon zest and cloves, if using. Dampen the edge of the dough with a little cold water. Roll out the remaining dough and carefully lay it over the apples. Press the edges together to seal and trim them with a sharp knife. Flute the edges.

Prepare the barbecue for 'Indirect heat' cooking, following the instructions on page 10.

Brush the pastry with milk and lightly dust with caster sugar. Make a small slit in the top of the pie to allow the steam to escape.

If using a gas barbecue, bake the pie at medium to high heat for 15 minutes and then reduce the temperature slightly to a low/medium heat and bake for a further 25 minutes or until the pastry is nicely browned. If using a charcoal burning covered unit, bake the pie for about 35 minutes at a medium to high heat (the heat indicator, if there is one, should register around 200°C/400°F). To test whether the pie is fully cooked, use a thin metal skewer to pierce, remove and check a piece of apple from below the steam slit.

Remove the pie from the barbecue, sprinkle lightly with more caster sugar and allow to rest for a few minutes before serving.

Pictured opposite:

Foccacia
Cheese & herb stuffed tomatoes
Roasted red peppers

Plain white bread
Cheese and herb rolls

Apple pie
Pizza mozzarella with tomato sauce

FruitsandPuddings

Aran rice pudding

A deliciously rich rice pudding - the skin (best part of the pud) caramelises to hide a creamy, gooey middle.

Serves 4-6

125g (4oz) short-grain rice, washed and drained

900ml (1¹/₂ pints) milk or a mixture of half water and half evaporated milk

50g (2oz) butter, plus extra for greasing

2 eggs

grated zest of ¹/₂ lemon

freshly grated nutmeg

Put the rice into a heavy based saucepan, add the milk, or water and evaporated milk, and bring slowly to just below simmering. Allow to cook on very gently for about 10 minutes or until the rice is barely tender.

Add the butter and sugar and stir until they have completely dissolved. Remove the saucepan from the heat and allow the contents to cool for 2-3 minutes.

Butter a 1 litre (1³/₄ pint) ovenproof pie dish.

Prepare the barbecue for 'Indirect heat' cooking, following the instructions on page 10.

Beat the eggs and lemon zest together and stir into the rice. Pour the mixture into the pie dish and sprinkle the surface with grated nutmeg.

Bake, with low to medium heat, for about 35-40 minutes (adding a few more minutes to the cooking time will give the pudding a thicker, creamier consistency, but over-cooking and/or using too high a heat may transform the pudding into something akin to a rice short-cake!).

Norman's 'naughty but nice' pineapple flambé

A sweet alternative use for the beverage that my friend Norman swears is best for keeping the blood in circulation, whilst standing up to one's thighs (occasionally armpits!) in the chilly waters of a salmon river.

Serves 4

1 ripe pineapple or 8 whole slices of canned pineapple

7 tablespoons clear runny honey

3 tablespoons white rum

clotted cream, or vanilla ice cream

If using a fresh pineapple, slice off the skin and cut out the fibrous centre. Slice the skinned pineapple across into 8 rings.

Prepare the barbecue for grilling, following the instructions on page 8.

Grill the pineapple rings over a high heat for 2-3 minutes each side whilst brushing frequently with the runny honey.

Place the hot pineapple on a serving dish and sprinkle over with the rum. Set the rum alight and serve immediately with clotted cream or vanilla ice cream.

BreadandPizza

Daily Bread

(pictured on page 137)

Surely there are few things that provides the cook with more satisfaction than the sight of freshly baked bread which they have personally conjured up. Without doubt the most evocative aroma that can pervade a kitchen is the smell of freshly baked bread. Why not, therefore, occasionally use your barbecue as an alfresco baker's oven and let your neighbours downwind share the enjoyment?

Apart from trying your hand at baking a standard white loaf, a recipe for which is on page 140, there is nothing to stop you tackling the more fancy shapes such as cottage, bloomer or plait; or indeed, using your yeast dough to bake the odd batch of sticky buns, light brioches or, perhaps more appropriately, tea-plate size burger-buns. A wide and interesting variety of packet bread mixes are readily available should you wish to cut a few corners.

Cheese and herb rolls

(pictured on page 137)

Makes 8

175g (6oz) butter, softened

125g (4oz) blue cheese, or grated Cheddar cheese

1 tablespoon finely chopped onion

1¹/₂ tablespoons chopped fresh parsley

1 teaspoon chopped fresh rosemary leafs

1 teaspoon dried basil

8 bread rolls, halved

Prepare the barbecue for grilling, following the instructions on page 8.

Cream together the butter and cheese and stir in the onion, parsley, rosemary and basil. Spread the mixture over the cut sides of each roll. Place the halves together and wrap each roll in aluminium foil. Place the rolls on the grill and heat through over medium to high heat for 12-15 minutes, turning once.

BreadandPizza

Plain white bread

(pictured on page 137)

Makes 2 loaves

750g (1½lb) strong white flour

1 teaspoon salt

1 sachet dried yeast

1 teaspoon sugar

425ml (13floz) lukewarm water

25g (1oz) lard, butter or margarine, plus extra for greasing

Pour about a third of the lukewarm water into a bowl, then whisk in the sugar followed by the dried yeast. Leave the mixture to one side to froth.

Meanwhile sift the flour and salt into a warm mixing bowl and rub in the lard, butter or margarine.

When the yeast is ready, make a well in the centre of the flour and pour in the yeast liquid followed by the remainder of the warm water.

Starting with a wooden spoon, then using your hands, work the batter into a spongy dough before turning out on to a floured surface. Knead well for ten minutes or so until the dough has developed a smooth sheen.

Return the dough to the bowl, cover with polythene or food-wrap and leave in a warm draught-free place, for 1-1½ hours until the dough has roughly doubled in bulk.

Turn out on to a floured surface and knead lightly for 30 seconds or so to expel the air from the dough.

Grease two 23 x 13 x 7.5cm (9 x 5 x 3 inch) loaf tins.

Divide the dough in half and make a loaf shape with each. Place in the prepared tins. Cover the tins with polythene or food-wrap (oiled on the underside to prevent the risen dough from sticking) and prove in a warm place for 20-30 minutes or until the dough rises just above the top of the tin.

Meanwhile prepare the barbecue for 'Indirect heat' cooking, following the instructions on page 10. If using a gas barbecue, and depending upon the barbecue's BTU rating, 'oven' capacity and the prevailing weather conditions, adjust the control knob to a position between medium and high so that the temperature indicator reads 220°C (425°F). If using a charcoal burning barbecue, create a normal fire which should result in a similar cooking temperature as above.

Place the proved loaves on the barbecue, and bake for 30-35 minutes until the loaves are well browned and shrinking slightly from the sides of the tin.

Tip the loaves out on to a rack and check that they are ready by tapping their bottoms; they should sound hollow. If the loaves appear somewhat pale on their base and sides, return them (out of their tins and upside down) to the barbecue for a couple of minutes to crisp up.

Foccacia
(Italian flat bread)

(pictured on page 137)

Goes well with summer salads, makes a great 'sponge' for mopping up juices and can be used for 'jaw-aching' sandwiches.

500g (1 lb) strong white flour

1 teaspoon salt

1 teaspoon sugar

1 sachet dry yeast

4 tablespoons extra virgin olive oil

about 250ml (8floz) lukewarm water

2 tablespoons olive oil

2 tablespoons sea salt crushed

fresh rosemary leaves

Mix the flour, salt and yeast in a bowl. Stir in the oil and most of the water to make a firm dough (add more water if required).

Turn the dough onto a lightly floured surface and kneed for 5-10 minutes until the dough is shiny, smooth and pliable. Place in a large, lightly oiled, bowl and cover with a tea towel or food wrap. Keep in a warm place (perhaps adjacent to the barbecue if it is lit) for about 40 minutes until the dough has roughly doubled in size.

In the meantime prepare the barbecue for 'Indirect heat' cooking, following the instructions on page 10.

Knock back the risen dough and roll out to a rectangular shape of about 30 x 20cm (12 x 8 inches) x 2cm (³/₄ inches) thick. Place on a well greased and floured baking sheet or fit into a greased and floured shallow baking tray. Return the prepared dough to the same warm place and leave about 10 minutes to rise.

Using the end of a wooden spoon handle or, Italian style, your little 'pinky' or index finger, make deep indentations over the entire surface of the dough.

Drizzle 2 tablespoons of oil over the dough and scatter with sea salt and rosemary leaves. Very lightly spray the surface with water.

Bake in the barbecue, at a moderate hot heat (about 200°C on the heat indicator) for about 25 minutes.

Best when served warm, or at room temperature.

BreadandPizza

Wholemeal rolls

Makes 12 rolls

1 teaspoon brown sugar

250ml (8floz) lukewarm water

25g (1oz) fresh yeast or
15g ($^{1}/_{2}$oz) dried yeast

500 (1 lb) wholemeal flour,
plus extra for kneading and dusting

1 teaspoon salt

50g (2oz) cracked wheat

Dissolve the sugar in a third of the lukewarm water and add the fresh or dried yeast. Mix well and leave, until foamy, in a warm place.

Mix the flour and salt in a large bowl. Stir the yeast mixture into the flour, gradually add the remaining water and mix with your hands to make a smooth dough. Knead the dough on a floured surface for about 5 minutes until it is elastic and no longer sticky.

Divide the dough into 12 pieces and shape into rolls. Place, spaced apart, on a floured baking sheet and leave to rise, covered with a damp tea towel. Leave in a warm place for 1-1$^{1}/_{2}$ hours or until nearly doubled in size. Prepare the barbecue for 'Indirect heat' cooking, following the instructions on page 10. If using a gas barbecue, and depending upon the barbecue's BTU rating, 'oven' capacity and prevailing weather conditions, adjust the heat control knob to a position between medium and high. The temperature indicator should read 220°C (425°F). If using a charcoal burning unit, create a 'normal' fire which should provide you with a cooking temperature similar to the one quoted above.

Sprinkle the rolls with the cracked wheat and place the baking sheet on the barbecue. Bake for 10-15 minutes or until the rolls are nicely browned.

Singin' hinnie

This traditional recipe hails from the North-East region of England where the phrase 'hinnie' (honey), is an endearment used by the men-folk when addressing their nearest and dearest. As for the 'singing' bit, this alludes to the sound made as the hinnie sizzles during cooking on the hot girdle (a flat iron baking plate with a curved handle). One could place a girdle, or thick-based frying pan, on the barbecue, but this recipe is formulated for units incorporating a griddle plate.

Makes 1, feeds 4–8

375g (12oz) plain flour

$^1/_2$ teaspoon salt

scant $^1/_2$ teaspoon bicarbonate of soda

1 teaspoon cream of tartar

75g (3oz) best lard

125g (4oz) currants

about 200ml (7floz) milk

Sift the flour, salt, bicarbonate of soda and cream of tartar together.

Rub in the fat and then add the currants. Mix to a soft dough with milk and turn out on to a floured surface and roll out to into a round roughly 1cm ($^1/_2$ inch) thick.

Prepare the barbecue for grilling, following the instructions on page 8.

Carefully place the hinnie on to the lightly greased griddle plate and bake, over a gentle to moderate heat, for about 5 minutes on each side (both sides should be nicely brown). When turning the hinnie, I suggest you use a couple of fish slices to deposit it on to a large plate, then having covered with a second plate, invert the plates and slide the scone back onto the griddle plate for further cooking.

Having removed the hinnie, let it cool slightly before splitting it with a long-bladed bread knife. Serve hot, (as you would a teacake) with lots of butter and jam.

BreadandPizza

Pizza dough

Your covered barbecue may be a mile away in resemblance to a pizzeria in a small Italian village, but the end result - smell, taste and bubbling surface, is not that far removed, aided by a little imagination, from the genuine article.

Makes 2 pizza bases,
each serving 2-4

15g (^{1}/$_2$oz) dried yeast

75-125ml (3-4floz) lukewarm water

250g (8oz) strong white flour or wholemeal flour, plus extra for dusting and kneading

1 teaspoon salt

1 egg, beaten

1 teaspoon oil

Mix the yeast with the water in a cup and stand it in a warm place for 10 minutes or until frothy.

Sift the flour and salt together in a mixing bowl. Pour in the yeast mixture and the beaten egg and mix, using one hand, to a scone-like dough that leaves the bowl clean, adding an extra drop or two of warm water if necessary.

Transfer the dough on to a floured work surface and knead for about 10 minutes until it is smooth and elastic. Return the dough to the bowl and rub the surface with the oil. Cover the dough with a clean, damp cloth and leave in a warmish place for about an hour, or until it has doubled in size.

Knead the dough lightly for a few minutes. It is now ready to shape into pizza bases.

Pizza mozzarella with tomato sauce

(pictured on page 137)

Serves 2-4

^{1}/$_2$ quantity of pizza dough (see recipe)

Tomato sauce:

2 tablespoons oil

1 medium-size Spanish onion, chopped

2 garlic cloves, crushed

2 x 425g (14oz) cans of Italian plum tomatoes

^{1}/$_2$ teaspoon dried basil

1 bay leaf

salt and freshly ground black pepper

Topping:

2 tablespoons oil

125g (4oz) mozzarella cheese, sliced thinly

50g (2oz) can of anchovy fillets, drained and roughly chopped

10 large black olives, stoned and halved

1 teaspoon dried oregano

1 tablespoon grated parmesan cheese

To make the sauce, heat the oil in a saucepan and fry the onion until soft and golden. Add the garlic, tomatoes, basil, bay leaf and salt and pepper to taste. Simmer over gentle heat for about 40 minutes or until the tomato mixture is thick. Remove the pan from the heat, discard the bay leaf and leave the sauce to cool.

Place the pizza dough in either one large, shallow pizza tin about 25cm (10 inches) square, or two small tins. The dough should line the bottom and sides of the tin.

Brush the dough with a little of the oil. Cover it with the tomato sauce and lay the cheese over the surface. Arrange the anchovies and olives attractively and sprinkle over the oregano and parmesan. Trickle the remaining oil over the top. Leave the pizzas for 15 minutes before baking.

In the meantime, prepare the barbecue for 'Indirect heat' cooking, following the instructions on page 10.

Place the pizza(s) on the barbecue. If using a gas barbecue, adjust the heat control knob to a position between the medium to high setting. Depending upon the power and size of the barbecue, and the prevailing weather conditions, a further adjustment may be required to bring the temperature reading to 220°C (425°F). If using a charcoal burning unit, create a 'normal' fire which should provide a good baking temperature. To check that the dough base is fully baked, lift an edge with a fish slice and take a peek.

Serve the pizzas straight from the barbecue, or cool on a wire rack to make this a delicious cold addition to a picnic meal.

Topping variations

Salami and mushroom topping

125g (4oz) salami or garlic sausage, cut into matchsticks

75g (3oz) mushrooms, sliced thinly

75g (3oz) tomatoes, sliced thinly

75g (3oz) mozzarella or Bel Paese cheese, sliced thinly

salt and freshly ground black pepper

Layer the salami or garlic sausage, mushrooms and tomatoes on top of the tomato sauce. Season with salt and pepper and cover with the cheese slices.

Smoked mozzarella and sun-dried tomatoes

175g (6oz) smoked mozzarella cheese, cut into 2.5cm (1 inch) cubes

150g (5oz) sun-dried tomatoes in oil, drained (reserve the oil) and roughly chopped

50g (2oz) mushrooms, sliced thinly

10 black olives stoned and sliced

1 tablespoons capers, drained

2 tablespoons torn fresh basil leaves

salt and freshly ground black pepper

1$\frac{1}{2}$ tablespoons tomato oil (reserved from the sun-dried tomatoes)

Scatter the mozzarella, sun-dried tomatoes, mushrooms, olives, capers and torn basil leaves over the tomato base. Season with salt and pepper, then drizzle the reserved tomato oil over the top.

Salads

Tomato and onion salad

This can be used as a tasty and refreshing starter, especially when served with some crusty French bread.

Serves 4

4 large or 6 small firm, ripe tomatoes, skinned and sliced thinly

2 medium-size onions, sliced thinly and separated into rings

1 teaspoon torn fresh basil leaves or $1/2$ teaspoon dried basil

2 tablespoons chopped fresh parsley

1 quantity of Vinaigrette dressing (page 147)

Arrange the tomato slices on a large flat plate. Try not to overlap the slices if you prepare the salad more than an hour before it is eaten because it tends to make the slices soggy. Scatter the onion rings over the tomatoes.

Sprinkle with the chopped herbs and drizzle over with the dressing.

Brown rice and vegetable salad

Serves 6-8

1 tablespoon groundnut oil

300g (10oz) brown rice

600ml (1 pint) boiling water

4 tablespoons Vinaigrette dressing (page 147)

2 large tomatoes, cut into thin wedges

$1/2$ red or green pepper, de-seeded and chopped finely

5cm (2 inch) piece of cucumber, chopped finely

1 medium-size red dessert apple, cored and chopped

1 small celery stick, chopped finely

2 tablespoons finely chopped spring onion or onion

25g (1oz) walnuts, chopped finely

25g (1oz) currants

salt and freshly ground black pepper

Heat the oil in a saucepan, add the rice and stir to coat all the grains. Add about 1 teaspoon of salt, pour over the boiling water and bring back to the boil. Stir once only, cover and simmer gently for 40 minutes or until all the liquid has been absorbed and the rice is bite-tender.

Empty the rice into a salad bowl and fluff it with a fork. Pour the prepared dressing over whilst the rice is still warm. Allow to cool.

When the rice is cold, stir in all the other ingredients, adding a little more dressing if desired, and season to taste. Keep the salad in a cool place until required.

Salade Niçoise

Prepare the salad as closely as possible to its serving time in order to keep the lettuce fresh and crisp.

Serves 4-6

1 firm round lettuce

3 firm tomatoes, skinned, de-seeded and quartered

$^1/_2$ small cucumber, peeled and cut into small chunks

1 medium-size red pepper, de-seeded and cut into narrow strips

2 spring onions, chopped finely

125g (4oz) French beans, barely cooked

2 hard-boiled eggs, quartered

50g (2oz) black olives, stoned

200g (7oz) can of tuna fish, drained well and broken into chunks

6 anchovy fillets, drained and halved lengthways

2 teaspoons capers (optional)

Vinaigrette dressing:

1 garlic clove, crushed

1 teaspoon sea salt

1 teaspoon mustard powder

1 tablespoon red or white wine vinegar

a pinch of freshly ground black pepper

6 tablespoons good quality green olive oil

1 tablespoon chopped fresh tarragon (optional)

First make the dressing. Using a pestle and mortar, pound the garlic with the salt until you have a smooth paste. Add the mustard powder, vinegar and pepper and mix thoroughly until the salt has completely dissolved. Add the olive oil and tarragon, if using. Pour the vinaigrette into a screw-top jar and, just before dressing the salad, give it a good shake to blend all the ingredients thoroughly.

Shake the lettuce dry. Remove the outer leaves and arrange around the base of a large salad bowl. Cut the heart into quarters and place on the base of the bowl. Sprinkle over a little of the dressing.

Arrange the tomato and cucumber pieces in layers over the lettuce with a little more dressing; then add the pepper strips, spring onions, and French beans. Top with the hard-boiled eggs, black olives and tuna fish.

Decorate the salad with the strips of anchovy fillet and the capers, if using. Spoon over more of the dressing and serve.

Caesar salad

Sometimes described as the classic American salad, this goes well with most barbecued food.

Serves 4

3 tablespoons lemon juice

2 tablespoons olive oil

2 tablespoons red wine vinegar

1 tablespoon Worcestershire sauce

4 garlic cloves, crushed

6 slices of white bread, crusts removed, cut into 1cm (1/2 inch) cubes

50g (2oz) butter

1 Cos lettuce

1 egg, beaten well or parboiled in its shell for just 2 minutes

50g (2oz) Roquefort or blue cheese, crumbled

50g (2oz) anchovy fillets, drained and cut lengthways into strips (optional)

salt and freshly ground black pepper

In a jug mix together the lemon juice, olive oil, vinegar, Worcestershire sauce and half the crushed garlic. Allow to stand for 4-6 hours. Strain to remove the garlic.

Toast the bread cubes on a baking sheet in a preheated moderately hot oven or on a preheated barbecue, stirring them occasionally until the cubes are lightly browned on all sides. Melt the butter in a large frying pan, add the remaining garlic and the toasted bread cubes and stir continuously until the cubes have absorbed the butter and are golden.

Separate the lettuce leaves, tearing the largest ones in half with your hands. Place the leaves in a large salad bowl. Pour the beaten or parboiled egg over the lettuce and add the dressing. Toss well until all traces of the egg disappear.

Add the crumbled cheese, anchovy fillets, if using, and bread cubes. Season to taste with salt and pepper and toss again.

Bean sprout salad with koi-kuchi-shoyu dressing

A colourful and delicious salad. ('Koi-Kuchi-Shoyu' is the Japanese phrase for regular soy sauce.)

Serves 4

125g (4oz) carrot, cut into matchsticks

250g (8oz) bean sprouts

2 small green peppers, quartered, de-seeded and cut into matchsticks

1 small red pepper, quartered, de-seeded and cut into matchsticks

2 teaspoons sesame seeds, toasted, (optional)

salt

Dressing:

3 tablespoons soy sauce

1 tablespoon olive or groundnut oil

2 tablespoons red wine vinegar

1 tablespoon sesame oil

First make the dressing by shaking all the ingredients together in a screw-top jar.

Bring 300ml ($^1/_2$ pint) of water to the boil.

Add $^1/_4$ teaspoon of salt and the carrot strips and blanch for 1 minute. Add the bean sprouts and peppers and, when the water simmers again, remove the pan from the heat. Drain off the water through a colander, compress the vegetables lightly to remove excess water and fan vigorously for 2-3 minutes to cool quickly.

Tip the salad into a large bowl, add the dressing and mix it all together gently.

Serve the salad in small individual bowls, leaving guests to sprinkle with the sesame seeds if desired.

Oriental cucumber and radish salad

Serves 4

12 fat radishes

1 small cucumber

Dressing:

1$^1/_2$ tablespoon soy sauce

$^1/_2$ tablespoon red wine vinegar

2 teaspoons sesame oil

$^1/_2$ teaspoon sugar

Cut the tops off the radishes. Crush each radish (use the side of a broad-bladed knife, or cleaver, for this task) to open it up whilst keeping it intact.

Cut the cucumber into pieces approximately 5cm (2 inches) long and gently crush. Cut the crushed cucumber lengthways into halves or quarters.

Combine all the ingredients for the dressing and mix well.

Arrange the radishes and cucumber pieces on a plate, pour over the dressing and serve.

Salads

Potato salad

Serves 4-6

1kg (2 lb) waxy potatoes with their skins on

$^1/_2$ teaspoon mustard powder

4 spring onions, chopped finely

150ml ($^1/_4$ pint) mayonnaise (see following recipe)

2 tablespoons chopped fresh parsley

paprika for sprinkling

salt and freshly ground black pepper

Boil or steam the potatoes in their skins until just tender. Drain, peel and dice them.

Mix the mustard and spring onions into the mayonnaise and add salt and pepper to taste.

Add the mayonnaise to the potato and mix gently with a spoon until it is well coated - this process is easier if the potatoes are still warm. Taste and adjust the seasoning if necessary. Sprinkle with the chopped parsley and a little paprika.

Mayonnaise

It is essential that the oil, egg yolk and wine vinegar are at normal (cool rather than warm) room temperature.

Makes about 150ml ($^1/_4$ pint)

1 egg yolk

$^1/_4$ teaspoon salt

$^1/_2$ teaspoon mustard powder

a pinch of freshly ground white pepper

150ml ($^1/_4$ pint) olive or vegetable oil

1 tablespoon white wine vinegar or lemon juice

Place the egg yolk in a bowl and very gradually beat in the salt, mustard and pepper. A wire balloon whisk is probably the best tool for this job; or use a small hand mixer or wooden spoon.

Add the oil, drop by drop, whisking vigorously after each addition. Once the mixture forms a shiny emulsion and has become thick (roughly half the oil will have been used), the oil can be added more quickly, say, 1 tablespoon at a time.

When the mixture is very thick, add the wine vinegar or lemon juice and mix in. Then blend in the remaining oil. The finished consistency should be similar to lightly whipped double cream. Taste and adjust the seasoning to your liking.

The mayonnaise can be stored in the refrigerator, in a covered container, for up to 2 weeks.

Note:

If you prefer to use a blender to make the mayonnaise, use a whole egg and add the oil in a thin stream with the blender set at a moderate speed.

Summerdrinks

There are no hard and fast rules on what libation to offer 'grown up' guests at a barbecue party but beer, lager and soft drinks apart, summertime drinks generally take the refreshing form of fruit cups and punches. Apart from being visually attractive and thirst quenching, cups and punches are generally low on stimulants and relatively inexpensive to make. A few recipes for fruit cups and punches are given but, as with barbecue sauces and marinades, I believe that making up one's own concoctions is far more satisfying: Mix them up well beforehand and keep, in bottles or plastic containers, in a cold box, together with lots of ice cubes – cold drinks should be served really cold!

What wine is best to serve and drink is a matter of personal taste, the main thing to remember is that it's there to be enjoyed. Although white wines seem the obvious choice for alfresco summer parties, there are several red wines that take kindly, indeed benefit, from being served lightly chilled, eg.

Lambrusco or a Rose. Blander food, such as chicken, go with a lighter wine such as Beaujolais, Valpolicella and Bardolino, whereas a superb roast beef should be accompanied with the best red wine you can afford. Having said that, it would, however, be quite sad to drink a top quality wine in the great outdoors. The finest nose would probably have great difficulty, to put it mildly, in capturing a fine wine's frail bouquet when competing with the garden's multiple natural aromas. Add the tangy pungent smells emanating from a barbecue in full cry and the battle would be truly lost, even before lips met glass and tongue tasted wine.

Should you need further help on what wine to buy for your next barbecue cook-out, simply browse the shelves in the wine section of your local supermarket or drinks store. All the wines on display will be fronted with a notice giving the wines characteristics, and price. If you need yet more assistance, seek out the person in charge who, hopefully, will be both a wine expert and a barbecue buff to boot.

Summerdrinks

Tangy-tomato cocktail

This makes a refreshing aperitif for a barbecue cook-out.

600ml (1 pint) tomato juice
300ml ($^1/_2$ pint) fresh orange juice
2 teaspoons caster sugar
$^1/_2$ teaspoon English mustard
pinch salt
pinch freshly ground black pepper

Place all the ingredients into a liquidiser and blend for 20 seconds or so. Chill well before serving.

Sangria

Serves 12

2 x 1 litre (1$^3/_4$ pints) bottles of red wine
1 litre (1$^3/_4$ pints) bottle of lemonade
4 tablespoons brandy
2 tablespoons caster sugar
1 large orange, cut into thin slices
1 large lemon, cut into thin slices
1 large eating apple, cored and cut into thin slices
ice cubes and soda water to serve

Pour the red wine, lemonade and brandy into a large jug. Add the caster sugar, orange, lemon and apple. Leave to macerate and chill in a refrigerator for 2-3 hours.

When ready to serve, add a tray of ice cubes, soda water to taste and stir well.

Kir

This makes a refreshing and elegant aperitif with which to welcome guests at a party.

To make, simply stir one tablespoon of cassis (blackcurrant liqueur) or raspberry or blackcurrant syrup into every glass of well-chilled dry white wine.

Summer cider cup

Serves 8

1 tray of ice cubes
grated zest of 2 lemons
1.2 litres (2 pints) cider
600ml (1 pint) soda water
1 tablespoon brandy
1 tablespoon Curacao
1 tablespoon Kirsch

Place the ice cubes in a large jug. Add all the remaining ingredients, mix well and serve immediately.

Hot spiced cider

Serves 12

This makes a nice warming drink for the grown-ups whilst they oversee the barbecue at the Halloween and Guy Fawkes festivities.

3.5 litres (6 pints) cider

10 cinnamon sticks

10 whole allspice

12 whole cloves

3 small pieces of fresh root-ginger

175g (6oz) brown sugar

Prepare the barbecue for grilling, following the instructions on page 8.

Put all the ingredients, except the sugar, in a saucepan. Place the saucepan in the middle of the grill, or on the side burner of a gas barbecue, and bring the contents to the boil. Stir in the sugar and allow the spiced cider to simmer for about 15 minutes.

Strain and serve hot.

Fruit punch

Serves 8

250g (8oz) sugar

300ml ($^1\!/_2$ pint) water

300ml ($^1\!/_2$ pint) fresh orange juice, chilled

300ml ($^1\!/_2$ pint) pineapple juice, chilled

600ml (1 pint) cold weak tea

2 tablespoons lemon juice

300ml ($^1\!/_2$ pint) ginger ale, chilled

sliced fruit in season, eg. 1 apple, 1 orange, 1 lemon and/or 1 passion fruit and $^1\!/_2$ pineapple

sprigs of fresh mint

6 strawberries, halved

crushed ice

Place the sugar and water in a saucepan and stir over low heat on the barbecue until the sugar has dissolved. Boil for 2-3 minutes. Cool and add the fruit juices, cold tea and lemon juice. Chill well.

Just before serving, add the ginger ale, sliced fruit, mint sprigs, the strawberries and crushed ice. Serve in chilled glasses decorated with more mint sprigs.

Marinades

The prime function of a marinade is to tenderise and enhance the flavour of cuts of meat that may be lacking in either or both departments. Like a skillful football manager, a good marinade can be instrumental in promoting a 'fourth division' cut of meat, into the 'third division'. Needless to say, there can be no substitute for prime quality, so whenever possible buy meat of the best grade (not necessarily of the highest price). In that way you are more than half-way to ensuring the best results in your cook-outs. The acid in a marinade, be it lemon juice, wine vinegar, wine or pineapple juice, acts as a tenderising agent; the fat (butter, oil or margarine) gives moistness to very lean meat and helps to protect the meat from losing too much succulence when cooked over high heat. If the marinade is acid, it is advisable to use a glass or china receptacle. If the meat is not fully covered by the marinade, it will be necessary to turn it occasionally. A good and easy way to turn food is to place both marinade and food in a strong plastic bag (or two just to be on the safe side) which is then tightly sealed. As an extra safeguard, place the sealed bag in a baking tin. Some foods can be left to marinate in the refrigerator for over 24 hours, whilst others only require a fleeting 'kiss'- say for 15 or so minutes. However, if marinating the food overnight in the refrigerator, remember to remove the food at least an hour before cooking.

Soy-sake marinade

Makes about 300ml ($^1/_2$ pint)

4 tablespoons soy sauce

4 tablespoons sake or dry sherry

3 tablespoons groundnut or sunflower oil

2 tablespoons clear honey

1 teaspoon freshly grated root ginger or a good pinch of ground ginger

1 garlic clove, sliced thinly

Combine all the ingredients and mix well. Use with red and white meats and fish such as salmon.

Sherry-ginger marinade

Makes about 150ml ($^1/_4$ pint)

4 tablespoons sweet sherry

2 teaspoons ground ginger

3 tablespoons soy sauce

1 tablespoon lemon juice

1 tablespoon brown sugar

2 tablespoons oil

salt and freshly ground pepper, to taste

Tabasco sauce, to taste (drop by drop)

Combine all the ingredients and mix well.

Use to marinate chicken, beef and spare ribs.

Soy-lemon marinade

Makes about 300ml ($^1/_2$ pint)

6 tablespoons lemon juice

6 tablespoons soy sauce

4 tablespoons groundnut or sunflower oil

1 teaspoon sesame oil

$^1/_2$ teaspoon freshly ground black pepper

1 garlic clove, crushed

1 bay leaf

Combine all the ingredients and allow the mixture to stand for at least an hour before use.

Excellent for joints of beef which can be left in the marinade (a strong well-sealed plastic bag is ideal for holding both joint and marinade) for up to three days in the refrigerator. The meat should be turned frequently and then drained well before roasting.

Teriyaki marinade

Makes about 150ml (¹/₄ pint)

1¹/₂ tablespoons clear honey

1¹/₂ tablespoons groundnut or
sunflower oil

4 tablespoons soy sauce

1 tablespoon dry red wine or
red wine vinegar

1 teaspoon freshly grated root ginger or
a good pinch of ground ginger

1 large garlic clove, crushed

Combine all the ingredients and mix well.

Use to marinate chicken, beef, spare ribs or fish.
Meat will need to be marinated for 4-8 hours or
overnight in the refrigerator - turn it
occasionally. Fish only requires marinating for
about 2-4 hours in the refrigerator. This also
makes a superb basting sauce. Try using it with
grilled salmon steaks.

Honey-mint marinade

Makes about 300ml (¹/₂ pint)

150ml (¹/₄ pint) dry white wine

4 tablespoons clear honey

1 teaspoon soy sauce

1 tablespoon chopped fresh mint

1 tablespoon red or white wine vinegar

1 garlic clove, crushed

1 teaspoon salt

Combine all the ingredients and mix until well
blended. Allow to stand for at least an hour
before use. Particularly suitable with lamb, but
can be used for chicken. Allow the meat to
marinate for 1-2 hours.

Marinade vin rouge

Makes about 450ml (³/₄ pint)

300ml (¹/₂ pint) dry red wine

6 tablespoons groundnut or
sunflower oil

50g (2oz) finely chopped spring onion

2 garlic cloves, crushed

1 teaspoon dried whole basil or oregano

1 teaspoon salt

¹/₂ teaspoon freshly ground black pepper

Combine all the ingredients in a heavy-based
saucepan and heat until the marinade starts to
simmer. Remove from the heat immediately,
cover the pan and leave for about 1 hour to cool.

Use with beef or pork.

Wine, oil and dill marinade

Makes about 150ml (³/₄ pint)

150ml (¹/₄ pint) dry white wine

3 tablespoons oil

1 teaspoon paprika

¹/₂ teaspoon salt

1 teaspoon sugar

a few sprigs of fresh dill

4 fresh chive blades, chopped

1 tablespoon very finely chopped fresh
parsley

a pinch of freshly ground black pepper

Combine all the ingredients and mix well.

This is particularly suitable for fish. Pour over
food and leave, covered and in a cool place, for
about an hour before cooking.

Sauces

The distinction between marinades and sauces can be somewhat blurred but, in general terms, a marinade is something that is applied to the food before cooking, and a sauce is something that is applied to the food during cooking and then consumed as part of the dish.

Sauces are best prepared in heavy-based saucepans and stirred with a wooden spoon. Most sauces, and certainly those incorporating sugar, honey or tomato, are best applied to the meat during the final 10 minutes or so of cooking. Applied too early and there is the likelihood that the surface of the meat will become unduly burnt.

Rich mustard sauce

Makes about 250ml (8floz)

100ml (3floz) sour cream

**2 tablespoons mayonnaise
(recipe page 150 or use shop-bought)**

**2 tablespoons mustard,
Dijon or wholegrain**

salt and freshly ground black pepper

Combine all the ingredients.

Serve with chicken or beef.

Chimchurri sauce

5 large ripe tomatoes

1 large onion

1 whole head fresh garlic

1 green chilli, de-seeded

a large handful of fresh coriander

125ml (4floz) extra virgin olive oil

125ml (4floz) red wine vinegar

salt and freshly ground black pepper

Place the tomatoes in a bowl and cover with boiling water. Leave for 2 minutes before draining and slipping off the skins (protect your hands when doing this). Cut the tomatoes open and remove their pips. Peel the onion and garlic cloves and rinse the coriander under running water to remove any grit.

Chop all the prepared ingredients finely, either by hand or briefly in a food processor, and place in a bowl. Stir in the oil and wine and season to taste.

Serve this fabulous sauce with any grilled meat or fish.

Salsa

2 tablespoons fresh coriander, chopped

**250g (8oz) ripe tomatoes,
de-seeded and diced**

1 small red onion, very finely chopped

juice of ½ lemon

**salt and freshly ground black pepper,
to taste**

Mix the salsa ingredients together and adjust seasoning to taste. Set aside for the flavours to blend.

Jim's new universal sauce

This makes enough to reserve some for future home cook-outs, or how about making up a fancy label and taking a jar in lieu of a bottle of wine or a 'six-pack', to an away cook-out.

Makes about 1.2 litres (2 pints)

2 tablespoons groundnut oil

2 garlic cloves, crushed

2 small green peppers, de-seeded and chopped finely

2 small onions, chopped finely

125g (4oz) celery, chopped finely

$\frac{1}{2}$ teaspoon dried basil

$\frac{1}{2}$ teaspoon dried thyme

$\frac{1}{2}$ teaspoon ground cinnamon

1 teaspoon salt

2 dashes of Tabasco sauce

$\frac{1}{2}$ tablespoon Worcestershire sauce

300ml ($\frac{1}{2}$ pint) water

450ml ($\frac{3}{4}$ pint) tomato ketchup

6 tablespoons red or white wine vinegar

1 tablespoon 'liquid smoke' (optional)

juice of 1 lemon

1 teaspoon grated lemon zest

Heat the oil in a large heavy-based saucepan and add the garlic, green peppers, onions and celery. Cook, over medium heat, for about 5 minutes, stirring frequently. Add all the remaining ingredients, except the lemon juice and zest, and cook for a further 5 minutes or so.

Add the lemon juice and zest and simmer, over gentle heat, for about 30-40 minutes, stirring occasionally towards the end of cooking. Add a little more water if the sauce is too thick.

Serve with chicken, pork, beef or fish.

Sweet and sour barbecue sauce

Makes about 300ml ($\frac{1}{2}$ pint)

250ml (8floz) tomato ketchup

150ml ($\frac{1}{4}$ pint) orange marmalade or apricot jam

2 tablespoons lemon juice

1 teaspoon Worcestershire sauce

1 teaspoon soy sauce

$\frac{1}{2}$ teaspoon horseradish sauce

$\frac{1}{2}$ teaspoon salt

a pinch of freshly ground black pepper

Put all the ingredients in a heavy-based saucepan and heat until simmering.

Serve with pork.

Honey and mustard sauce

Makes about 250ml (8floz)

6 tablespoons clear honey

3 tablespoons English or French mustard

$\frac{1}{2}$ teaspoon horseradish sauce

1 tablespoon cornflour

3 tablespoons red wine vinegar

2 tablespoons lemon juice

Put all the ingredients in a heavy-based saucepan and cook over gentle heat, stirring continuously, until the mixture clears and thickens slightly.

Serve with hamburgers, steaks and chops.

Sauces

Rich Chinese sauce

Makes about 450ml ($^3/_4$ pint)

6 tablespoons soy sauce

4 tablespoons clear honey

1 tablespoon soft brown sugar

$^1/_2$ teaspoon curry powder

$^1/_2$ teaspoon ground ginger

1 large garlic clove, crushed

$^1/_2$ teaspoon salt

a pinch of freshly ground black pepper

3 tablespoons preserved ginger, drained well and chopped finely

6 tablespoons dry or medium dry sherry or dry white wine

Combine the soy sauce, honey, sugar, curry power, ground ginger, garlic, salt and pepper in a heavy-based saucepan and, over gentle heat, bring it to the boil, stirring continuously.

Draw the pan to one side and stir in the preserved ginger and the sherry or wine. Reduce the heat and simmer for 5-10 minutes, stirring until the sauce thickens.

Serve with chicken, pork or beef.

Indonesian sauce

Makes about 300ml ($^1/_2$ pint)

1 tablespoon oil

4 tablespoons smooth peanut butter

150ml ($^1/_4$ pint) tomato ketchup

3 tablespoons Worcestershire sauce

garlic powder to taste

$^1/_4$ teaspoon salt

Heat the oil in a heavy-based saucepan and add the peanut butter. Cook over gentle heat, stirring occasionally, until the peanut butter thickens and darkens slightly. Remove the pan from the heat immediately and stir in the tomato ketchup and Worcestershire sauce.

Season the sauce to taste with garlic powder and the salt. Allow to stand for 2 hours before use.

Reheat the sauce gently and add a little water if the sauce is too thick.

Serve with chicken and steaks. It can also be used to baste chicken.

Jim's jammy-ginger sauce

Makes about 350ml (12floz)

500g (1lb) apricot jam

4 tablespoons dry white wine, or white wine vinegar

2 tablespoons melted butter or oil

1 tablespoon freshly grated root ginger or $^1/_2$ teaspoon ground ginger

$^1/_2$ teaspoon salt

Combine all the ingredients in a heavy-based saucepan and heat until simmering, stirring occasionally.

Serve with chicken and pork.

Soy, orange and wine sauce

Makes about 450ml (³/₄ pint)

4 tablespoons soy sauce

6 tablespoons orange juice

6 tablespoons soft brown sugar

150ml (¹/₄ pint) dry white wine

¹/₂ teaspoon mustard powder

¹/₂ teaspoon ground ginger

2 dashes of Tabasco sauce

2 shallots, chopped finely

a pinch of ground cinnamon

3 tablespoons water

2 teaspoons cornflour

salt and freshly ground black pepper

Combine all the ingredients, except the cornflour and seasoning, in a heavy-based saucepan and bring slowly to the boil, stirring continuously. Allow to simmer for about 5 minutes. Stir in the cornflour to thicken. Season to taste with salt and pepper.

Serve with chicken and pork.

Lily's luxury tomato sauce

Makes about 250ml (8floz)

1 tablespoon extra virgin olive oil

15g (¹/₂oz) butter

1 medium-size onion, finely chopped

1 garlic clove, crushed

1 teaspoon dried mixed herbs

125ml (4floz) tomato purée

2 large ripe tomatoes, skinned and roughly chopped

2 teaspoon balsamic vinegar

salt and freshly ground black pepper

Heat the oil and butter in a heavy-based saucepan and add the onion, crushed garlic and mixed herbs. Cook for about 3 minutes or until the onion has softened. Stir in the chopped tomatoes, tomato purée and balsamic vinegar and continue cooking for a further 4 to 5 minutes, stirring occasionally. Remove the pan from the heat and allow to cool. Place the sauce in a food processor and liquidise until smooth. Season the sauce to taste with salt and freshly ground pepper.

Serve warm or cold with hamburgers, sausages, steaks, chops and fish.

Flavouredbutters

Flavoured butter can be made up seven to ten days before use, as long as it is kept in the refrigerator in a covered dish. Remove the flavoured butter from the refrigerator and then melt and brush it on to the food; or place a piece of the butter on the second side of the meat during the final two minutes of cooking and allow it to melt. Some of the butters also make tasty and economical sandwich spreads. The 'use with' suggestions are not to be treated as sacrosanct so please mix and match as you see fit.

To prepare the following butters, beat the butter until soft; then add and thoroughly mix in the other ingredients. Using wet hands, shape into a roll about 4cm (1$\frac{1}{2}$ inches) in diameter. Wrap gently in foil and chill well. Keep in the refrigerator until ready to serve. All the butters are suitable for freezing.

Lime and dill butter

1 teaspoon lime zest
2 teaspoons lime juice
$\frac{1}{2}$ teaspoon finely chopped fresh dill
$\frac{1}{4}$ teaspoon freshly grated root ginger
125g (4oz) butter

Use with seafood, poultry and vegetables.

Mustard and onion butter

2 tablespoons Dijon mustard
1 tablespoon finely chopped
spring onion
1 garlic clove, chopped very finely
$\frac{1}{4}$ teaspoon freshly ground black pepper
a dash of Worcestershire sauce
125g (4oz) butter

Use with red meat and duck.

Lemon and parsley butter

2 tablespoons lemon juice
1 teaspoon finely grated lemon zest
1 tablespoon dry white wine (optional)
1 tablespoon finely chopped fresh
parsley
125g (4oz) butter

Use with seafood, poultry and vegetables.

Garlic butter
(medium strength)

1 garlic clove, chopped very finely
1$\frac{1}{2}$ tablespoons chopped fresh parsley
125g (4oz) butter

Use with seafood, red meat, vegetables and French bread.

Blue cheese butter

75g (3oz) blue cheese, crumbled finely

1/4 teaspoon paprika

1 garlic clove, chopped very finely

1 tablespoon finely chopped spring onion

125g (4oz) butter

Use with red meat (including hamburgers). It also makes an excellent filling for baked potatoes.

Herb and garlic butter

1/2 teaspoon dried tarragon or rosemary

1 tablespoon finely chopped fresh chives

1 tablespoon finely chopped fresh parsley

1 garlic clove, chopped very finely

1/4 teaspoon salt

a pinch of freshly ground black pepper

125g (4oz) butter

Use with poultry, seafood, vegetables and French bread.

Tabasco and lemon butter

2 teaspoons Tabasco sauce

1/2 teaspoon lemon juice

a pinch of salt

Use with seafood and poultry.

Maitre d'hotel butter

2 teaspoons finely chopped fresh parsley

1/2 teaspoon salt

2 teaspoons lemon juice

1/4 teaspoon dried thyme

a pinch of freshly ground black pepper

125g (4oz) butter

Use with vegetables and fish, or as a baste for chicken.

Orange and honey butter

1 tablespoon fresh orange juice

1 tablespoon finely grated orange zest

1 tablespoon clear honey

2 teaspoons finely chopped fresh parsley

125g (4oz) butter

Use with lamb, duck, chicken and turkey.

Tarragon and parsley butter

1/4 teaspoon dried crushed tarragon

1 tablespoon finely chopped fresh parsley

1/2 teaspoon grated lemon zest

2 teaspoons lemon juice

1/4 teaspoon salt

125g (4 oz) butter

Use with red meat, especially steaks.

Such is the huge range and diversity of barbecue equipment currently available, one can readily appreciate why coming to a decision as to which model to purchase, proves a little difficult for some people. Judging from the comments of hundreds of men and women I have talked to at my barbecue cookery demonstrations, it would appear to be a problem roughly comparable to the dilemma facing many ladies when buying a new dress, or cosmetic, and men, including yours truly, when having to select a new tie or birthday present for their nearest and dearest!

Bearing in mind that some barbecues are very similar in price to various major household appliances, such as dishwashers and refrigerators, it obviously makes sense to carry out some basic research before setting out for the barbecue emporium. Your choice will narrow considerably if, for example, you decide beforehand which fuel, be it gas, charcoal or wood, best serves your needs. Some thought should also be given as to the prospective barbecue's size, and its capability, in handling the *normal* demands that will more often than not be placed on it. Also, and very important, what cooking techniques is it your intention to pursue? If your fancy leans toward roasting and smoke-cooking meats, baking bread, pies etc, then you will require a barbecue with a lid. If, on the other hand, your culinary ambitions stop short at grilling fast-cooking foods such as burgers, cutlets, chicken portions, fish etc, then barbecues such as the 'Braziers' and 'Flat Tops' (see over) will fully meet the bill. Talking about 'Bills', it is probably a good idea to set yourself a budget to work to, which should include, if you are starting out from scratch, such items as tools, accessories and of course fuel and firelighters.

Charcoal burning barbecues

Charcoal and wood-fuelled barbecues can be roughly divided into two categories:

Portable

These models are designed for use away from the home-base by picnickers, backpackers, campers, caravanners and the like.

For those travelling light, such as walkers and cyclists, the economically priced '*Disposable*' barbecues are the practical choice simply because of their compact size and light weight. Disposable units, normally available in 2-3 sizes, comprise a shallow foil tray housing a quantity of lumpwood charcoal (adequate to provide 20-30 minutes cooking time), a sheet of lighting paper and a grill made from a piece of expanded metal. Although termed 'Disposable', these very handy little barbecues can be re-fuelled, and placed in a carrier-bag (to prevent the charcoal dust from spreading) for further use. Next in line in this category, are the *Picnic barbecues*. There are many models, and ingenious designs, to take your pick from. Some are rectangular in shape, others circular, with one brand new model sporting a triangular shaped fire-bowl. Most picnic barbecues are simply scaled down versions of their larger brethren, incorporating similar features such as windshields and adjustable grills. Some of the larger models have lids which, whilst providing shelter to food that is being grilled on a windy day, is very limiting when it comes to roasting and baking food by 'Indirect heat' (see page 10). Picnic barbecues that come supplied with fold-down, or clip-in legs, are far more comfortable to work with, and therefore a little safer, than those 'legless' models that have to be set down on the ground. Finally, in this general category and deserving a mention by themselves, are the ubiquitous **Hibachis**. In days past, the word hibachi epitomized the art of barbecuing (the word, of Japanese origin, means fire-box, fire-bowl, or, simply, brazier). Sizes can vary from a mere 10-12cm (4-5 inches) to a circular version around 41cm (16 inches in diameter). Up to 30 years or so ago, hibachis were made solely from cast-metal but nowadays they are available in cast-metal and pressed steel.

'Stay At Home' barbecues

The phrase indicates those models that appear destined to spend their life at their owners residence. **Brazier barbecues;** the name speaks for itself in that these are 'open-top' units. Like their smaller cousins they can be either rectangular or round shaped, with, or without, wheels and made from sheet or cast metal. Braziers invariably incorporate a windshield specifically designed to support a rotisserie. Some models incorporate a food grill which rotates freely on an axis but with most models the food grill has to be adjusted by moving it into variable height slots on the face of the windshield. **Flat Top barbecues** now occupy a very significant and fast growing segment of the 'open top' category. Unlike the Braziers, some of which can be fairly easily dismantled and transported, 'Flat Tops' are destined, because of their weight and bulk, to spend the whole of their working life at their home-base. With their cast iron grills and griddle plates, set in a sturdy hardwood trolley, these heavy-weight units are strikingly similar in looks to their gas-burning brothers (see below). They incorporate full-width easy removable ash pans, adjustable charcoal baskets (for heat control) and large wheels and casters for ease of manoeuvre. **Covered barbecues**. For those cooks with culinary aspirations far beyond the limitations inherent with an open barbecue, a barbecue with a vented lid is required. Barbecues that

have a lid can be used, with great success, to roast and bake a wide and interesting variety of food. However, for many people, the main advantage that a covered barbecue has over an open unit (and very certainly over a kitchen-bound oven) is that it can be used for solely **Smoke-cooking** meat and fish (see page 11). One of the most popular covered barbecues around is the **Kettle**. The spherical-shaped version of the kettle has a grill and grate that sit in a permanently fixed position. The grill on the square-shaped kettles can however be adjusted to various heights and, very usefully, different inclinations. Some square kettle models also incorporate a rotisserie. The largest units in the 'covered barbecue' category are the **Wagons**. Like their 'lidless' cousins, the 'Flat Tops', the bigger Wagon barbecues can comfortably cope with the 'flat food' (burgers, steaks etc) demands of large parties and/or large joints of meat. Certain ultra heavyweight wood-burning models, easily recognised by their distinctive smoke-stacks and large 'Wagon wheels', reminiscent of the wonderful smoke-puffing steam-engines, with their cow-catching buffers, that have been featured in countless 'Westerns', are capable of handling and smoke-cooking very large quantities of food. These barbecues, known as 'Pit Barbecues' in the USA, are now available in Europe. Apart from the smallest 'Wagon', most models have a **Heat indicator** mounted in their lids. These gadgets are very useful in that they make baking and roasting a more precise exercise than would be the case if carried out in a covered barbecue minus a heat indicator. Virtually all 'Wagons' incorporate a **Warming rack**, an exceedingly useful item. Retractable racks, ie. those that swing back with the lid, when opened, are for me far more 'user-friendly' than racks set in a permanently fixed position. **Built-in charcoal barbecues** are readily available in DIY kit form. The basic kit usually comprises a chrome-plated food grill, fire-grate, ash / fat tray and support brackets. Kits are supplied with detailed instructions on how to build a rectangular-shaped supporting brick structure, usually requiring around 100 bricks to complete. Tips on the design and location of an 'Outdoor barbecue cooking area' are set out on page 182.

Check-list for charcoal-burning barbecues

- To check the stability of the barbecue on display, bearing in mind it will, at some stage, have to support a fully laden grill, plus a charcoal fire-bed, give the assembled unit a nudge to see if it oscillates unduly. Note: a 'wobble' could well be due to a display unit's poor assembly, so do take that into account.

- If the barbecue has a chrome-plated food grill, check that it has no thin or bare patches.

- If the barbecue has an adjustable-height food grill that is supported by the windshield (the deeper the windshield the better), check that the grill slots easily into the shield, again bearing in mind that the grill will, at some stage, be fully laden and heavy to handle.

- If buying a covered barbecue, check that its lid fits neatly and is not distorted. Ensure that the lid's air vent(s) can be easily adjusted.

- If the barbecue has a mechanism for raising and lowering the food grill, check that it operates smoothly and positively.

- Are the grill bars spaced closely enough to stop food, such as small sausages and chicken wings, falling through?

- Make sure that there are no sharp edges to the barbecue's lid, fire-box or ash pan.

Gas Barbecues

Gas barbecues enjoy several advantages over their charcoal-burning brethren whilst, at the same time, producing food that tastes, looks and smells just the same as that created by charcoal barbecues. Not surprising perhaps, bearing in mind that the 'barbecue hallmark' is in fact created by the food itself ie. as the radiant heat (from whatever source*) strikes the food, the savoury juices released by the food vapourise and the resultant smoke haze rises up to embrace the food, to impart the distinctive taste, appearance and aroma so beloved by barbecue aficionados all over the world.

*Most gas barbecues utilise a single layer of long-lasting lava-rock, or ceramic briquettes, as their heat bed. There are however models where the traditional rock/briquettes heat bed has been supplanted with vitreous enamelled steel sections, cast metal hearths or, in the case of a unique kettle design, a large vitreous enamelled steel cone.

Gas barbecues can be used with either butane or propane gas, but because the operating, pressures for the two different types of gas are different, it is very important to use the correct regulator. Suffice to say, it is not possible to change from one gas to the other without also having to change the regulator.

Gas barbecues... the benefits:

- They are easy to get going, even in windy conditions, in that most have push-button or rotary Piezo spark ignition. Conversely, after cooking has been completed, they are just as readily turned off. This latter asset is, in my personal opinion, of particular importance when considering the unnecessary waste of energy that only too often occurs when a charcoal fire-bed is left alone, after completion of cooking, to extinguish itself an hour or so later.

- They are ready for use only 5-10 minutes after ignition. This helps enormously in that it leaves the cook/host in a more relaxed state of mind when having to juggle fire-lighting, with getting the food, drink, etc, all together in the hectic run-up to the party.
- They are very economic, fuel-wise, to use. This can create a potential problem in that a cylinder of gas appears to be everlasting, particularly if the barbecue is being utilised on relatively few occasions throughout the year. Sod's law dictates that the gas will run out soon after you start cooking. So beware!
- Cooking heat is easily and precisely controlled by adjusting a knob (rather than by raising and lowering the food, or charcoal grills or opening and closing air vents.)
- They are, to a fair degree, self cleaning (see page 180).

Gas barbecues can be divided into two categories:

Portable

Like their charcoal counterparts, portable gas barbecues are eminently suited for holiday use, but even more so due to the added bonus that they can be pressed into service, at the drop of a hat, for general cooking duties eg. boiling a kettle and frying breakfast. Models vary considerably in weight, power, design and cooking capacity. The lightweight units are, in general, powered by universally available disposable gas cartridges. The smallest cartridges provide approximately $1\frac{1}{2}$ hours of cooking time. Most portable units can, however, be hooked up to standard gas cylinders which are greatly more economic to use.

'Stay At Home'

Gas barbecues in this category, due to their greater bulk and weight, will normally remain tied to their owner's abode.

Flat Top gas barbecues are rapidly increasing in popularity amongst the world's barbecuers. At first glance they appear very similar to their charcoal-burning cousins, but of course display 2, 3 or 4 burner control knobs. Like the charcoal units, they also feature cooking surfaces split between a cast metal grill and cast metal griddle (usually a $^{50}/_{50}$ or $^1/_3$ - $^2/_3$ split). The multi-burner format, coupled with multi-purpose cooking surfaces, make this type of gas barbecue a highly versatile unit. A pull-out, full width, drip tray, positioned in the base of the barbecue, ensures that the patio surface etc is kept grease-free. A flat, full size lid is provided to protect the cooking surfaces and burners from bad weather, and free from the attention of marauding cats etc.

Note: Some *'Flat Tops'*, can be converted to a Wagon (covered) barbecue by fitting a *'Roasting hood'*.

Wagon Gas Barbecues, like the charcoal burning models referred to above, come in a wide range of sizes and cooking capacities. The smallest units (from what is termed the 'Table Top' family) have a cooking area of around 32sq ins (200sq cm) and the largest up to a massive 640sq ins (4000sq cm). Apart from the smaller models, most Wagon gas barbecues have a 'Heat Indicator' mounted in their lids and embody a *'Warming Rack'*. Power ratings vary from 11,000 BTU (3 kilowatts) to 50,000 BTU (14.5 kilowatts).

Burners are to gas barbecues as engines are to cars. As with anything else, you usually get what you pay for, so be aware that there can be a big variation, from the burners of one gas barbecue to another, in terms of quality, performance and durability. Some Wagon gas

165

barbecues have, in addition to its main burners, a burner that is mounted adjacent to the hood. These very useful outside burners, usually referred to as *Side-burners* allow the cook to prepare soups, vegetables, sauces, hot drinks etc whilst grilling, roasting or baking is taking place on the adjacent grill. For me, however, a side burner, the more powerful the better, makes the ideal location to mount a small Wok and indulge in a bout of Stir-frying, Braising, Deep-frying or Steaming. Hints on how to use your gas barbecue for Wok cooking are given on page 14. Another auxiliary burner that one occasionally comes across in the more expensive Wagon units is the *Rotisserie burner*. Located at the rear of the grill area, the heat radiating from the burner impacts the rotating meat from behind, thus allowing the fats and juices to fall freely and directly into a drip pan. A further advantage that these units have is that one can spit-roast with the hood of the barbecue in the shut position, which is a great deal more efficient, particularly during windy conditions, than is the case when spit-roasting with an open unit.

For some barbecue enthusiasts the idea of installing a **Built-in Gas Barbecue** in a garden landscape has considerable appeal. The concept first became popular in California during the 1950s, when many of the dwellings built during that period invariably incorporated an outdoor cooking and eating area in their overall design. Perhaps the use of the word 'permanent' is a little misleading in that whilst the structure (usually brick or stone) within which the barbecue sits, is certainly permanent, the barbecue itself is removable for winter storage unless, that is, one is contemplating, quite rightly, using the facility all year round. Gas barbecues that are destined for the above use, range from Wagons (minus their under carriage) to the Flat Tops (minus their trolley).

Check-list for Gas Barbecues

▌ Check that the barbecue has been 'CE Approved' (for the European market) or by the official approval authority in North America and other countries throughout the world. The barbecue should carry a sticker to that effect. If in doubt, check the barbecue's safety and technical credentials with the retailer.

▌ Are the burner controls conveniently situated?

▌ Check the barbecue's stability. If one of the heavy units, can it be fairly easily manoeuvred? **Warning**: Never attempt to move a gas barbecue when its burners are alight.

▌ Has sufficient volcanic rock or ceramic briquettes been provided? There should be enough to cover the fire-grate in a single crowded layer. Note: A smallish gap around the perimeter of the grate is OK, but largish gaps could permit fats to descend directly onto the burners which could, perhaps, result in a flare-up.

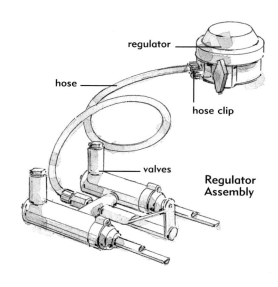

regulator

hose

hose clip

valves

Regulator Assembly

Tools and Accessories

In keeping with the fun nature of barbecuing, some tools and accessories may appear to border on the frivolous. All of the items featured below can, however, be considered useful to the barbecue cook. Novice barbecue cooks, if they have to make a choice, should concentrate their attention on those tools that help to make barbecuing easier and safer. Tongs, gloves and forks being the first tools to obtain. Other tools and accessories can be added later.

Apron and Gloves

For comfort and practicality, nothing, in my opinion, beats a cotton apron. It should be long enough to cover one's knees and ideally have a couple of deep pockets in the front in which to stash a roll of kitchen towelling, matches etc. From clammy experience, I can assure you that wearing a plastic-coated apron whilst standing over a hot barbecue, is tantamount to spending time in a sauna, whilst wearing an overcoat! Buy gloves rather than mitts, and gauntlets rather than gloves, because wrists and the lower forearm need some protection too! The glove's design should allow tools to be gripped firmly and comfortably and the fabric, coupled with the heat resistant padding, give effective protection against the barbecue's considerable radiant heat.

Basting Brushes

Long-handled basting brushes are readily available but some barbecue cooks like to copy professional chefs and use a couple of good quality 5cm (2 inches) paint brushes, one to apply the oils and the other for applying sauces. The brushes' bristles should be natural; nylon and other man-made fibres are unsuitable.

Bug Repellents

Bug repellents, in spray or citronella candle form, are worth having around for warm summer evenings when biting, flying insects are attracted by the party lights. If you happen to live in a low-lying area, where such insects fly around in squadrons, you might perhaps consider investing in an electronic 'bug zapper' (similar to those found in food establishments). Depending on the model, areas up to two acres, so it is claimed, will be kept free of the dreaded mosquito family if one of these gadgets is installed and operating.

Chopping Boards

The larger the board is, the better. Ideally they should be made from one of the new laminates but a good quality hardwood board will suffice, providing it is scrupulously cleaned immediately after every cook-out.

Cleaning Brushes

The problem, as I see it, with most grill cleaning brushes, useful as they undoubtedly are, is that after relatively little use their fine wire bristles invariably clog up with fat and food debris. This then leaves you with the messy task of cleaning the cleaning brush! A cheaper alternative by far, which I find quite satisfactory, is the 'Foil ball' mentioned below. The metal scraper blade, which most brushes incorporate, is very handy for scraping off the burnt-on fatty deposits from the upper and lower housings of the barbecue and for doing likewise with a greasy griddle plate.

Drip Pans

Roasting meat by the 'Indirect heat' method (see page 10 for further information) is a cooking technique that all owners of covered barbecues will become very familiar with. For

167

most covered units, this method of cooking calls for a drip tray to be placed immediately underneath the area of the grill where the meat or poultry is to be sited. A drip pan, so positioned, catches the falling fats and juices thus helping to keep the base of the barbecue in a cleaner state than otherwise would be the case. A standard steel roasting tin used as a drip pan, will require cleaning out and washing at the completion of every cook-out otherwise, if left, could start to become noisome. One can purchase lightweight drip pans made from aluminium. These, presumably, are meant to be discarded after just one outing (they do not stand up particularly well to being scrubbed clean more than once in my experience), but for lazy, mean-minded cooks, like me, making a drip pan from a roll of aluminium foil is profoundly more satisfying and rewarding. It not only saves me money, but it allows me to skip the

irksome cleaning task referred to above. Incidentally, it is much easier to remove the pan from the barbecue for 'binning' once its fatty contents have been allowed to partly congeal.

To make a drip pan from foil

Take a 46cm (18 inches) roll of heavy-duty foil and tear off a strip about 10cm (4 inches) longer than the length of the proposed pan. Fold the foil in half lengthways, double-fold the edges to make 2.5cm (1 inch) walls, flatten the foil walls and lightly score a bisecting line at each corner. Pull out and pinch the corners (as shown in the diagram) before folding them tightly back against the sides. The result should be a leak-proof pan approximately 13cm (5 inches) wide with walls 2.5cm (1 inch) high. To create a wider and larger pan, use wider foil or simply fold the foil widthways.

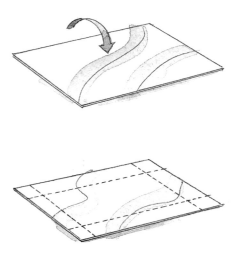

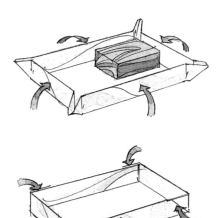

First Aid Kit

Suffering the small burn and blister is par for the course during a busy barbecue year. A spray-on burn lotion would therefore make a useful addition to your home first aid kit.

Foil

Aluminium foil, as previously mentioned, is indispensable to the barbecue cook. Try to purchase the 'heavy duty' foil rather than the more flimsy variety, especially if it is your intention to make your own drip pans. Foil can also be used for wrapping and cooking vegetables and fruit, protecting the protruding bits of poultry, fish etc, making a temporary griddle plate and, when crumpled into a ball, use to remove burnt-on food deposits from grill bars, spit rods and metal skewers.

Forks

Not much to say about these except they should be long-handled with a comfortable wooden or PVC grip.

Gas Lighters

Also known as Gas Matches, these products are particularly handy for owners of gas barbecues that do not incorporate a Piezo igniter. In fact they are well worth having around as a stand-by for those who own units that do have this excellent gizmo. Gas lighters are also very effective for getting solid firelighters going, lighting garden flares etc.

Hinged Wire Broilers

Chrome-plated hinged wire broilers come in many different shapes and sizes. The square, rectangular or round broilers are excellent for handling quantities of chicken wings, cocktail sausages, chicken livers and the like that are small enough to fall through the grill bars of some barbecues. It therefore follows that the bars of the broiler should themselves be closely spaced. Broilers used in this fashion are very handy in that one can turn over several pieces of food at one time and, providing the bars of the broiler have been well oiled, it is far less likely that the food will stick to the barbecue's grill bars. Some broilers have pockets shaped to accommodate up to half a dozen burgers or chops. These can also be pressed into service for toasting bread, burger buns etc.

Particularly useful are those designed to hold fish - which can be particularly fragile to handle when partially cooked and needs turning. Usually referred to as fish holders, the most common will accommodate a single fish, such as a trout, weighing up to around 375g (12 ounces) with the largest single fish broilers able to hold a fish weighing in at around 1kg (2 lb). Another version that is available, will hold three fish, each around 375g (12 ounces), side by side. Sardines are pernickety to handle, but there is a broiler, looking something like a bicycle wheel, that can contain up to 12 of these little fish. Finally there are the cylindrical or rectangular box-shaped broilers which, when clamped to a spit rod, allows small pieces of food eg. chicken wings, to tumble about freely as the spit rotates.

Kitchen Paper

Apart from makeshift napkins, a roll of absorbent paper towelling, has many other uses. Handily slung from the cook's waist by a piece of string, pieces can be torn off to be used for mopping up spills, mopping brows, spreading oil over fish and grill bars, just prior to placing the fish on the grill, wrapping around hot sausages etc to protect guests' fingers and the wiping of children's runny noses!

Knives and Cutlery

A good quality 'butchers' knife is required for trimming and portioning meat. A small paring knife will also be required for preparing fruit and vegetables and a sharp carving knife is essential for tackling roasts. Most, if not all, of the above knives will probably come from the kitchen drawer.

We all know that cutting through a less than tender steak or a carbon-coated sausage, whilst balancing a plastic plate on one's lap, can be a daunting, and inevitably messy, task. In these circumstances anything less than really sharp steak knives will not do. Fortunately much of what is cooked and served at a typical barbecue is finger food, but if plastic cutlery has to be used, try to avoid the really 'cheap and nasty' variety which always, for me at least, seems to break into small pieces on first coming into contact with the food!

Meat Thermometers

A meat thermometer helps to take the guesswork out of cooking large joints, particularly useful when checking if a joint of pork is fully cooked. Meat thermometers are generally available in two styles: those with the round, clock-face with its moving hand that broadly tells you if the meat you are cooking is rare, medium or well-done, and the arrow-shaped thermometer that has a column of mercury from which the meat's inner temperature can be read. With either type, a false reading will occur if the tip of the pointed probe touches bone or spit rod. *Do not leave* the thermometer in the meat during the cooking process as the glass may shatter and, anyway, the face of the thermometer will quite quickly become coated with burnt fat and thus prove very difficult to read.

Paint Scrapers

These are the professional's choice for removing food debris and fat from griddle plates. Do not be tempted to use your old paint 'paint scraper', but buy one to reserve for culinary use only.

Pots and Pans

Pans should have long handles which, if wooden or plastic, can be given some protection from the heat, when the base of the handle is directly over the barbecue's grill, by wrapping them with foil. The pans should preferably have thick bases and, for the sake of domestic harmony, a pan or two, solely for barbecue use, should be purchased.

Skewers

Metal skewers with a flat, or twisted, blade are best for spearing chunky pieces of meat and/or vegetables. Round, small diameter skewers tend to leave the food behind when turned. The best skewers for holding food firmly in position are the twin-pronged versions reminiscent, perhaps, of ladies hair-grips. Most of the longer skewers have wooden or PVC handles. Bamboo skewers, traditionally used for satay and small appetisers, should be well soaked in water before use to prevent them burning up before the food is fully cooked.

Rotisseries

Whilst relatively few barbecues come supplied with a rotisserie (also known as a Spit-roast assembly) as standard, most barbecue manufacturers do however include a rotisserie set in their range of accessories. Virtually all charcoal Brazier models have windshields that will accommodate a rotisserie. The bottom casing of all Wagon gas barbecues are designed to do likewise. The vast bulk of spit-motors are battery operated, the most efficient of which work off two HP2 batteries. The plastic housing of the single-battery motor is very vulnerable to the effects of the heat emitted from the barbecue. Wrapping two or three layers of foil around the casing beforehand will help to prevent 'meltdown'. Badly balanced food on the spit-rod will result in the motor undergoing excessive wear. Apart from carrying out the spit-balance test (see page 12) the best solution is to use a set of balance weights. Using an adjustable weight when spit-roasting an irregular shaped joint, such as a leg of lamb, will ensure a smooth rotation and thereby help to reduce wear and tear on the motor. You may however have a little trouble in tracking a set of weights down.

Spatulas

Used mainly for turning over flat items of food such as burgers, spatulas should be long-handled with a broad slotted blade to allow some of the food's fat to drain through. The scissor-action of twin-bladed spatulas allows the cook to grip and position the food more easily than the single-bladed version.

Tongs

A pair of tongs is, without any shadow of doubt, the single most important tool in the cook's arsenal. It is therefore well worth taking the trouble to seek out a set that not only suits your strength of hand but will allow you to manoeuvre, and cleanly pick up a chipolata, even a stray baked bean, without the tongs 'crossing their legs' and catapulting the food at some innocent bystander! A good, pre-purchase, test is to pick up a pencil. The 'mouth' of the tongs should gently, but firmly, grip the food - sharp teeth may pierce the sealed surface of the food and allow some of the precious juices to escape.

Woks

A wok and a gas barbecue constitute the ideal cooking partnership. Almost equally so with a charcoal barbecue providing the barbecue's shape, and area of fire-bed, is adequate to fully seat the base of the Wok on, or very near, the fire-bed. More about the wok and wok-cooking on page 14. When purchasing your wok, try to include a set of wok tools ie. a ladle and a 'shover' (depicted in drawing below).

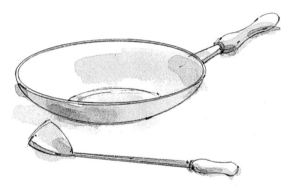

Safety first

Gas Barbecues...some Do's & Don'ts

After assembling your new barbecue, your first task *before* commencing to use it, is to spend time reading and inwardly digesting the notes, set out in the manufacturer's operating manual, on safety and how to get the best use from your unit. Safety really should be first, and 'Christening' your new barbecue should come second!

Here are a few basic 'do's' and 'don'ts'

▌ *Do carry out a leak test* before fitting the hose, valve and regulator (all of which are normally supplied interconnected), although, with some models, you may be required to supply and fit the regulator to the barbecue's control panel.

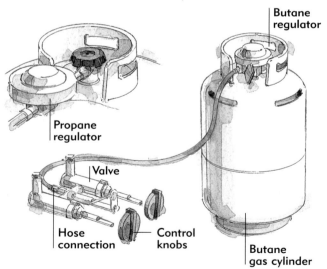

Butane regulator

Propane regulator

Valve

Hose connection

Control knobs

Butane gas cylinder

To carry out the test:

1. Make up a soap and water solution.
2. Take your full gas cylinder and the hose, valve and regulator assembly to an outside area and connect the regulator to the cylinder valve.

3. Turn the control knob(s) of the barbecue valve(s) to the 'Off' position.
4. Turn the gas supply on at the cylinder.
5. Apply soapy mixture to all the connection points, from, and including, the cylinder. valve to the valve(s) at the end of the hose.
6. Check each connection point for bubbles caused by leaks. Tighten any leaking connections (any item that persistently leaks must be replaced).
7. Turn off the gas supply at the cylinder and turn the control knob(s) to the 'High' position to release the pressure in the hose. Disconnect the regulator from the cylinder and fit the assembly to the barbecue following the manufacturer's instructions.

▌ Do make sure that you have a means of lighting the gas before turning on the supply.

▌ Do fully close the cylinder valve when the barbecue is not being used.

▌ Do store the cylinder outdoors in a well-ventilated place.

▌ Do keep the cylinder upright at all times.

▌ Do ensure that the lid of the barbecue is open before lighting the gas burners.

▌ Do allow at least 75cm (30 inches) of space between the barbecue and any flammable material (wood etc).

▌ **Do keep children and pets well away from all hot barbecues.**

▌ Don't store the cylinder of gas in direct sunlight.

▌ Don't smoke or use a naked flame when testing for gas leaks!

▌ **Don't store or use petrol, or any other volatile liquids or vapours near the barbecue!**

▌ Don't adjust your gas barbecue indoors or in any confined, unventilated area.

▌ Don't move a gas barbecue when it is lit.

Getting All Fired Up

Fuel, Firelighters and Firemanship

Fuel

Leaving gas-burning barbecues to one side, experienced practitioners of the art will tell you that the success, or otherwise, of all cook-outs hinges on the quality of the fuel being used. Charcoal can vary enormously in this respect so before blaming yourself, or your equipment, for an unsatisfactory performance, you might consider whether the charcoal itself was up to scratch. If in doubt, try another brand and, if necessary, keep doing so until you find one that meets the bill ie. is relatively easy to get started, provides an excellent level of heat and, if briquettes are your choice, is long burning.

Lumpwood charcoal

This is charcoal that comes straight from the kiln in lumps, of varying sizes, which are then broken up into graded pieces deemed suitable for barbecuing. Good-quality lumpwood charcoal should be bone-dry and feel light for its bulk. There should be a minimum of dust and very small pieces lying in the bottom of the bag. The best quality lumpwood charcoal is made from hardwoods (beech etc) but it is not uncommon for some softwoods to find their way into the kiln. It takes roughly 6 tons of green wood, plus a lot of labour and skill, to make just 1 ton of charcoal. Lumpwood charcoal's main advantage is that it is relatively easy to light.

Charcoal briquettes

All briquettes are made from pulverised materials – be it 100% hardwood char, a mixture of hardwood char and mineral carbons or (in the case of one very popular Australian brand) the product is made from mineral carbon which burns hotter and longer. A starch, or similar, compound is used to bind the pulverised material into pillow-shaped briquettes. Roughly speaking, briquettes burn for about twice as long as lumpwood charcoal which makes them particularly suitable for tackling long-cooking large roasts. Due to their dense composition, briquettes can sometimes prove difficult to ignite. 'Instant-lighting' charcoal, which is now universally available, can be ready for cooking over some 20 minutes after the paper bag it is packed in, is lit. Note: Never add this form of charcoal to an established fire as the fumes given off in the early stages will adulterate any food on the grill.

Wood

'Pit barbecues', mentioned earlier under 'Equipment', can consume fairly large amounts of hardwood during a busy season. Virtually any hardwood, providing it is well-seasoned, can be used, with beech probably being the most readily available followed by oak, birch, ash, apple and cherry. Vine cuttings are easy to light, but you will require a goodly amount to produce sufficient cooking heat, for even a relatively short time, which tends to limit its use to fast-cooking food such as small fish, cutlets, chicken wings etc.

Firelighters

Warning: *Never use petrol, methylated spirits, lighter fluid, kerosene, naptha or similar volatile liquids to light your fire.* **IT IS DANGEROUS TO DO SO – BOTH TO YOU AND THOSE STANDING BY!** *Never add more starter fluid, of any kind, to a charcoal or wood fire which has already been ignited – even if it does not appear to be burning. Should you wish to rekindle the fire, use a solid firelighter. If in any doubt, it is safer to start the fire again from scratch.*

173

Solid firelighters

Widely used for many years to start the home fires burning, the familiar solid white block has become equally popular with the barbecue fraternity. Unfortunately, when it has been lit, this traditional firelighter emits a rather unpleasant odour combined with a certain amount of black smoke. However, both the smoke and the odour will have dissipated well before the fire is ready to cook over. A 'smokeless' version of the solid firelighter is however available which is non-toxic, odourless and clean burning.

Liquid firelighter

Commercial liquid firelighters specifically sold for barbecue use are non-volatile, but nevertheless should not be added to a lit fire.

Jellied alcohol (lighter paste)

Somewhat expensive for home-based barbecues, but a very convenient starter for picnic barbecues.

Gas torch

Good results can be achieved with a compact gas torch as used for DIY jobs around the house, and by chefs for putting the finishing touches to crème brulee, but it does require the user to be on hand for a few minutes until the fire gets hold.

Charcoal chimney

A charcoal chimney comprises a metal tube, handle attached, roughly 15cm (6 inches) in diameter and 30cm (12 inches) long. Having placed the chimney on the barbecue's grate, the bottom of the tube is stuffed with two or three crumpled sheets of newspaper, plus perhaps a few small pieces of kindling . The chimney is then filled with charcoal and the paper lit. Once the charcoal has ignited, it should take only 15 minutes or so, carefully

remove the chimney and spread out the coals as required.

'Firemanship'

The launch pad for a successful barbecue cook-out is a well-made fire.

Preparing a charcoal fire-bed for: Grilling, Wok cooking or Griddle plate cooking

First build a pyramid-shaped pile of charcoal in the centre of the fire-grate.

If using solid firelighters, insert two or three pieces well into the lower half of the pile. After lighting, the starter will burn for about 15 minutes depending on the type of barbecue and wind strength. When most of the coals are covered by a grey ash, spread over the grate (if wok-cooking, leave the pyramid intact) one layer deep, and leave alone until the coals are completely covered in ash. You can now start to cook. TIP: During the early stages of fire-lighting, particularly if the wind is up, keep an eye on the pieces of firelighter to make sure they are burning well and have not gone out.

If using liquid firelighter, follow the manufacturer's instructions carefully. Take care not to use too much liquid, particularly with barbecues that incorporate air vents in their fire-bowl as excess liquid may drain out of the barbecue and accidentally ignite.

If using jellied alcohol, squeeze small amounts of jelly into cavities near the base of the charcoal pyramid. Close and remove tube, and light the jelly as soon as possible.

If using a gas torch, arrange the charcoal on the grate one layer deep and closely together. Light the gas and adjust the flame, and then play the flame slowly over the fuel until grey patches appear.

For Spit-roasting

Position a pile of charcoal on the fire-grate towards the rear of the fire-bowl and light as described above. The spit-roast cooking technique is covered on page 12.

Spit-roasting meat on the barbecue using a drip pan

For Roasting, Smoke-cooking & Baking by 'Indirect Heat'

(applicable only to covered barbecues eg. 'Kettles')

Having ensured that the barbecue's lower vents are fully open, place a pan (an old roasting tin will suffice) in the centre of the fire grate or, if your unit is a round 'kettle' model, clip its charcoal retention rails into position. Place two solid firelighters, about 10 cm (4 inches) apart, on each side of the grate. Having covered the firelighters with the required number of briquettes (for your first attempt at 'Indirect Heat' cooking, around 40 briquettes per side should prove adequate to tackle the Sunday roast), light them with a long match or taper. The time it will take for the fire to become established could vary from 30 minutes to 60 minutes depending on the number of firelighters used and wind strength. ie. if you are in a hurry, double up the firelighters. The 'Indirect heat' cooking technique is covered on page 10.

Heat control

When the fire-bed has been prepared, and the fire is making steady progress, you are left free to concentrate your attention on cooking the food and controlling the heat. Controlling the heat that emanates from a charcoal-burning barbecue is not as simple, or precise, as the instant control achieved with a gas barbecue. One can, however, adopt the following methods:

(a) by adjusting the lower air vents in a covered barbecue (the vent in the lid of a covered barbecue should always be left open during cooking);

(b) by altering the distance between fire-bed and food grill by means of rotating grills, adjustable levers etc;

(c) by increasing or decreasing the distance between individual briquettes, or pieces of lumpwood charcoal, once they are alight: the closer the lumps of fuel, the more intense the resulting heat;

(d) food is cooked by the infra-red radiation given off by the hot coals, so anything that masks the radiation will slow down the cooking process. Periodically tapping off excess ash (rapping the rim of the barbecue's fire-bowl should do the trick) will produce a small surge in temperature - conversely, leaving the ashes *in situ* will help to dampen an over-hot fire.

▌ If you are engaged in a protracted 'open-grill' cooking session, keep a reserve of briquettes around, but not quite touching the live coals. Cold briquettes, when added directly to hot coals will, momentarily, dampen down the fire whereas pre-warmed briquettes, when nudged up against hot coals, will not produce such an adverse effect. The other benefit is that unused charcoal can be retrieved at the completion of the cook-out for future use.

175

'Flaming Flare-ups!'

Some barbecue cooks believe a flare-up (sudden blaze) is a cross that all who stand at the helm of a barbecue, have to occasionally bear and put up with. Some people are in fact convinced that a mighty flare-up is an essential element in the barbecue ritual due to them seeing, in books and magazines, photographs of food-laden barbecues with flames (usually phoney) leaping skyward. However, apart from those cooks who actually set out with intent to flame-cook, my advice is to avoid flare-ups like the plague! One of the problems with a flare-up is that it can, unless you react fast, quickly spoil the appearance of the food. Chicken portions, on their way to becoming 'cremated', get covered in a black, greasy film, which requires wiping clean with kitchen paper before carrying on cooking. The worst flare-ups are created by excessive heat striking excessively fatty food. Unless one reacts very smartly, the fat raining down onto the fire-bed will quickly boost the flames into a mini-inferno. It would, however, be virtually impossible to avoid creating a flare-up, even using a fairly moderate cooking heat, if the entire grill was completely covered with fatty food such as sausages, burgers, chicken portions or lamb cutlets etc.

How to avoid flare-ups with charcoal units

Regardless of the quantity of food that has to be barbecued, refrain from covering all of the grate with charcoal because, in the event of a flare-up, there would be no alternative but to remove all food from the grill. The answer is to use a pair of tongs to set out the hot coals in the manner shown in the drawing ie. cover roughly one-third of the grate with charcoal that is crowded closely together, roughly one-third where the charcoal briquettes, or pieces of lumpwood, are set about 5cm (2 inches) apart and the remaining area of the grate left completely devoid of fuel.

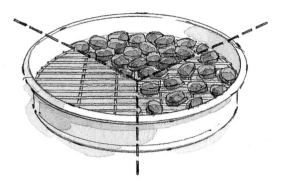

The layout suggested above can of course be modified, but it could be particularly useful when having to tackle a batch of steaks where each guest demands a different degree of doneness for their steak ie. the surfaces of the steak can be quickly sealed over the 'Hot Spot' before moving it to the adjacent 'Moderate Heat' sector. The fully cooked, or partly-cooked steaks can be 'parked up' over the 'Vacant Lot'. Using the above set-up, you should, with a little practise, be able to rustle up rare, medium and well-done steaks to order, with everyone tucking into their steak at the same time.

- By tilting the barbecue slightly toward the 'Vacant Lot', with grill bars facing in the same direction, some of the fat and juices from the food will trickle down the bars to drop off into a pre-positioned drip pan.

- Before grilling spare-ribs or pork cutlets, seal them with two or three tablespoons of water in a foil package and heat in a moderate oven (or in a covered barbecue) for about 40 minutes. This will render out a lot of the fat thus considerably reducing the possibility of a flare-up, and greatly shortening the cooking time. Another fat/flare-up-reducing exercise, when confronted with the prospect of barbecuing a large quantity of chicken pieces or large sausages, is to place them in a roasting tin, cover loosely with foil and gently sweat in a moderate oven or covered barbecues (using 'Indirect heat') for about 30 minutes or so. In losing a good deal of their fat, the chicken drumsticks etc will take on a somewhat lacklustre appearance but will regain their good looks during subsequent grilling. Try to conduct the above exercise as close to the cook-out as possible and remember to keep the part-cooked food covered, and in a cool place.

Snuffing out the fire

One of charcoal's great attributes is that it will, once lit, carry on steadily burning until it has been reduced to a grey ash. This however, is particularly wasteful, in every sense of the word, if there is still a goodly amount of solid coals left when cooking has been completed. With covered barbecues, the fire can be snuffed out by closing the top and bottom dampers. The hot coal should be extinguished in about 30 minutes. With open models the coals can either be carefully transferred to a lidded metal coal bucket, or dumped into a pail of water for later draining and drying. **Never** pour water over the hot coals when they are sitting in the barbecue. Doing so could badly damage the unit.

Gas Barbecues

'Troubleshooter'

Burners will not light

Possible cause: The cylinder of gas is almost empty
Solution: Replace with a full cylinder.

Possible cause: The cylinder valve is not fully open
Solution: Fully open the cylinder valve (turn the valve anti-clockwise).

Possible cause: The valve outlets are not properly seated in the venturi
Solution: Fully locate the valve in the venturi (when properly in position, the gas jets are visible through the 'window' in the venturi).

Possible cause: One or more of the gas jets or venturis is clogged (perhaps with spider webs or cocoons – quite possible if the barbecue has not been used for some time)
Solution: Clean the inside of the venturi tubes with a bottle brush. Carefully clean the jet orifices with fine wire or the tip of a round toothpick – do not enlarge the hole.

Possible cause: The venturis are not properly seated
Solution: Check that the retaining spring, if used, is properly engaged.

Possible cause: A sharp kink in the flexible gas hose
Solution: Re-position the cylinder to straighten the hose.

Possible cause: The igniter is not working
Solution:

a) Check the assembly instruction to ascertain if the gap between the electrode cover is correct (if it is correct, a spark should be visible);

b) Ensure that all wires are intact and connected;

c) Check the ceramic component for cracks (if a new igniter assembly is required, use a long taper in the meantime).

Possible cause: A defective valve or regulator
Solution: If you suspect either of the above items are faulty, remove the hose from the barbecue and take it, along with the regulator and cylinder, to an authorised servicing bottle gas dealer for inspection.

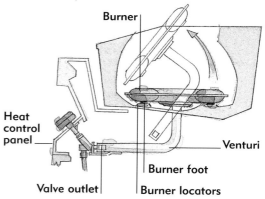

Burners provide insufficient heat

Possible cause: The barbecue is not given sufficient time to warm up
Solution: Increase the warm up time by several minutes to allow for low air temperatures and strong breezes.

Possible cause: The venturis and gas jets are not properly aligned
Solution: Fully locate the valve in the venturi.

Possible cause: Some of the vents in the burner assembly are clogged with food debris
Solution: Brush clean (using a brass or stainless steel bristle brush).

Possible cause: An excessive amount of volcanic rock is used
   Solution: Remove sufficient rock to allow a close-packed single layer only.

Possible cause: One, or more, of the gas jets or venturis is clogged
   Solution: Clean the inside of the venturi with a bottle brush. Carefully clean the jet orifices with fine wire or the tip of a round toothpick.

Possible cause: The volcanic rock is heavily permeated with food debris and fat
   Solution:
   a) Wash the rocks in hot water to which a biological soap (powder, tablet) solution has been added. Change the water and repeat as necessary. Make sure the volcanic rock is thoroughly dry before using for cooking. Dry it either in the barbecue with the lid down or in the kitchen oven.

   b) Alternatively, burn the rocks clean – see care and cleaning on page 180.

Flashback
(flame in or around the venturi)

If flashback should occur, immediately shut off the barbecue burner controls and then the cylinder valve off.

Possible cause: The venturis have become blocked when the barbecue has cooled
   Solution: Clean the inside of the tube with a bottle brush

Possible cause: The venturis are not properly seated
   Solution: Check that the retaining spring (if used) is present and engaged

Possible cause: The valve outlets are not properly seated in the venturi
   Solution: Fully locate the valve in the venturi.

Possible cause: The vents in the burner assembly are clogged
   Solution: Brush clean, using a brass or stainless steel bristle brush (if a wire brush is unavailable, clear the blocked vents with a piece of fine wire or a round toothpick).

Possible cause: The barbecue is exposed to strong winds
   Solution: Shield the middle/lower half of the barbecue from the wind (or turn off the gas and move the barbecue to a more sheltered position).

Burner flame is excessively yellow

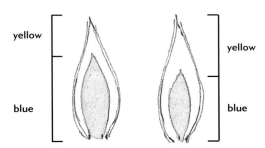

yellow

blue

yellow

blue

Possible cause: The burner holes are clogged
   Solution: Brush clean with a brass or stainless steel bristle brush.

Possible cause: The venturis tubes are blocked
   Solution: Clean the inside of the venturi tube with a bottle brush.

Possible cause: The venturis are not properly located on the valve outlets
   Solution: Check that the retaining spring, if used, is properly engaged.

179

careandcleaning

Care & cleaning

All barbecues, be they charcoal, wood or gas-fired, tend to become somewhat gungy after only a few cook-outs. Hygienic considerations apart, allowing your barbecue to get progressively dirty makes it increasingly less efficient. It therefore pays to get into the habit of giving the food grills and, if the unit has one, the griddle plate, a basic clean after every cooking session. There are a variety of ways to tackle the job. Some people have adopted the **'wet newspaper'** method. This involves spreading several sheets of newspaper on the ground, and giving them a good soaking, before laying the grills (which should preferably still be warm) on top. Having placed a few more sheets of paper over the grills, these also should be soaked. The theory has it that when the grills are removed, some hours later, the encrusted fat and food debris will be left behind (some might say appropriately) with the newsprint. Using a **wire brush** is the most preferred method, but brushes with fine wire bristles, can become clogged fairly quickly and thus, themselves, require laborious cleaning. My personal preference is simplicity itself: loosely crumple up a good size piece of aluminium foil and, with gloved hand, press the ball of foil firmly down onto the warm grill bars, scrubbing along the line of bars to remove all the food encrustations. A quick wipe over with some kitchen paper and the barbecue is ready for its next outing. During the next warm-up you can, if you wish, give the bars a further wipe-over with kitchen paper but in the meantime the heat will have acted as an effective cauterant. If you have a large sink (a shallow seed tray or something similar will do) then giving the grill an occasional soak in hot water, in which biological soap (powder or tablet) has been dissolved, should produce sparkling results.

Gas barbecues

Giving the grills and fire-bed (volcanic rock or ceramic briquettes) on your covered gas barbecue a basic clean after every cook-out is easy and straightforward ie. having removed all the food from the grill, and with the barbecue still alight, close the lid and adjust all the burner controls to the 'High' setting. Leave the barbecue for 5-10 minutes, which should be long enough for most, if not all, the fat and food residues to burn off the grills and some of the fats to burn out of the rocks. Be warned however that during the first few minutes of 'burn off' a considerable volume of smoke could issue from under the lid so make sure that doors and windows are closed, or well up wind of the barbecue! The alternative method, carried out just prior to lighting up, is to turn over all the cold rocks or briquettes and add an extra minute or two to the warm-up period. A perfect way to kill two birds with one stone!

Annual spring clean

It does not necessarily have to be undertaken in springtime, but giving your gas barbecue a thorough cleaning once or twice a year (twice if you are an 'all year rounder') will help to keep your unit in tip-top working order. Proceed as follows:

1. Remove the food grills, volcanic rocks, or briquettes, burner and ignitor assemblies.
2. Cover the valve outlets with aluminium foil.
3. Scrape and wire brush the inside surfaces of the barbecue's upper and lower housings to remove food debris. Clean off the surface with hot water and mild detergent using a scrubbing brush or scouring pad.
4. Brush the surface of the burners with a wire brush. Clean out any clogged vents with a piece of stiff wire.

5. Remove the foil from the valve outlets, clean the jet orifices (using fine wire) and replace the burner (ensuring the valve outlets are inside the venturi), and the ignitor assembly. Replace the grate, rock, or briquettes.

6. If the barbecue has a window in its lid, clean the glass (when it is cold) using hot water and a mild cleanser. Do not use a commercial oven cleaner.

7. Clean and treat any wood shelving and support structure with an approved wood preservative.

8. Clean the food grills as described above.

9. Clean out the drip pan or drip tray.

10. Finally tighten up all nuts and bolts in the frame assembly.

Tricks of the trade

Taking your gas barbecue's 'Heat fingerprints'

Burner configurations on gas barbecues vary quite considerably from manufacturer to manufacturer. Small portable units, and the smallest Wagon models, have a single rectangular-shaped burner, usually referred to as a 'Ribbon burner', positioned in the centre of the lower casing. The shape of burners in Wagon gas barbecues can vary from a squared figure of eight to an H-shape. ' Flat Top' gas barbecues invariably have multiple, evenly spaced, narrow ribbon burners made from cast metal. The shape, size and location of the barbecue's burners (in relationship to the cooking area they are serving), together with their power output, greatly influences the manner and speed in which the food is cooked.

Experience will eventually make you aware of where the 'Hot', 'Less hot' and 'Cool' spots on your barbecue grill are, but an easy, and tasty way to ascertain the heat distribution pattern

of your new gas barbecue (its 'fingerprints') is to conduct:

'Uncle Jim's Toast Test'

For this you will require a loaf of sliced white bread. Try to choose a calm day, or a sheltered spot, to conduct the test – preferably around tea time.

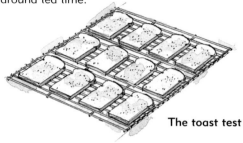

The toast test

1. Light the burners in the usual manner. If your unit is one of the covered models, close the lid.

2. Leave the barbecue to warm up for about ten minutes.

3. Adjust the control knob(s) to the Medium heat setting and leave for a further 2-3 minutes.

4. Having opened the lid, should there be one, completely cover the surface of the food grill(s) with slices of the bread and leave for about two minutes or until the underside of the bread is nicely browned.

5. Using tongs, turn each slice of bread in situ. to reveal, by the gradation of the breads colour, where the grill's hottest and coolest areas are.

In order to gain maximum kudos from the above highly scientific test, I suggest that you finish off toasting the bread, lavishly anoint the crisp golden slices with butter and strawberry jam (topped with a big dollop of thick cream?), before dishing out the 'naughty but nice' slices to a highly appreciative family. It's a great way to start building up your alfresco culinary reputation!

181

A few tips on constructing an Outdoor Barbecue Cooking Area

An ideal time to quietly sit down and plan a barbecue area, is when your new garden landscape is being prepared, or an existing garden layout is being altered. Should the former be the case, and it happens to coincide with a new dwelling in the course of construction, so much the better, as this will provide you with the satisfying opportunity to 'freeload' matching bricks and materials to build the barbecue's support structure.

Using organic stone for the structural framework has its drawbacks in that it can prove somewhat difficult for the amateur bricklayer to work with. In addition, natural stone could also appear to be somewhat incongruous when standing alongside brick, and stand out like the proverbial sore thumb. The same comment could also apply to a structure made from, say, red housing bricks set against the backdrop of warm honey coloured stone walls. Many people, quite wisely, opt for reconstituted stone blocks which are readily available, reasonably cheap to buy and fairly simple for the handyman to work with. Considerable care should be taken over the barbecue's design, layout and location, because errors at this stage may not be easy to rectify at a later date, particularly if it involves digging up concrete foundations and knocking down a solid brick or stone edifice!

Careful consideration should be given also to the work surface immediately adjacent to the barbecue itself. Ideally, it should be of a size adequate to comfortably accommodate chopping boards, tools, condiments and serving dishes. For those going the whole hog, there could also be a separate work surface for use by the 'commis cook' (deputy chef) to prepare salads etc. Cupboards, set underneath the work surface, whilst not essential, again would be useful for storing fuel etc or, out of season, gardening equipment.

Should it be your intention to hold 'evening into night-time' barbecue parties it makes good sense to grab the opportunity, at the pre-construction stage, to have a power cable laid to the barbecue area. This, however, is a job for a competent electrician to tackle - it is better to be safe and sure. Having had the power cable installed, you will then be able to mount at least one spotlight covering the general area around the barbecue, particularly important if there are hazards present in the shape of steps, ponds, prickly bushes, bird baths, statues etc. Equally, if not more important, is having a spotlight positioned directly above the barbecue to enable the cook to at least discern whether the food on the grill is in a burnt or unburned state. If there is to be only one light source, avoid positioning it directly behind the cook as doing so will only make matters worse by the creation of a deep shadow over the barbecue's cooking surface.

For the sake of good hygiene, there should be two buckets of hot water, plus a bar of soap, nail-brush and towels, handily placed for the cook and his helpers to use. The water should be regularly renewed during the cook-out. However, where expense is no object, a small sink with running water (bliss for blistered fingers!), somewhere adjacent to the work surface, would be a very useful luxury.

If there is adequate space, insert four small concrete bases in the ground around the perimeter of the barbecue area on which to mount the legs of a garden canopy. Apart from keeping the cook, food, and helpers dry in wet weather (coping with a batch of burgers with one hand, whilst the other hand is grasping an umbrella, is not an easy task). A canopy will also shelter the cook and helpers from the sun's rays.

If the built-in barbecue has to be located fairly close-up to the house, try to ascertain, prior to commencing work, how the wind generally behaves in that particular spot bearing in mind if French doors or windows are accidentally left open during cooking, they could act as a conduit for aroma rich smoke to permeate throughout the house. This could well result in your furniture, furnishings and resident pets, taking on a 'Smoky barbecue' flavour!

Turf will become quickly worn and increasingly slippery, particularly in the early evening, when subjected to heavy foot traffic. So for safety's sake, the area immediately surrounding the cooking and serving points should be either paved with non-slip concrete slabs or covered with a roughened concrete or gravel surface. Finally, do site the barbecue well away from tree and shrubs - in fact any flammable material.

cookingtimes

Roasting (using 'Indirect heat')

Food	Cut	Degree of Cooking	Heat Setting	Internal Temperature	Approximate Minutes per 500g (I lb)
Beef	rib-roast	rare	low/medium	75°C/140°F	18-20
		medium	low/medium	85°C/160°F	20-25
		well-done	low/medium	90°C/170°F	25-30
	sirloin		medium	75-90°C/140-170°F	25-30
	rump/rolled		medium	80-90°C/150-170°F	25-30
Lamb	leg	rare	medium	75°C/140°F	18-22
		medium	medium	85°C/160°F	22-28
		well-done	medium	90°C/170°F	28-33
	crown roast	rare	medium	75°C/140°F	25-30
		medium	medium	85°C/160°F	30-36
		well-done	medium	90°C/170°F	36-42
	shoulder	medium	medium	85°C/160°F	22-28
		well-done	medium	90°C/170°F	28-33
Pork	loin	well-done	low/medium	100°C/185°F	25-30
	fresh ham	well-done	low/medium	100°C/185°F	20-25
	crown	well-done	low/medium	100°C/185°F	25-35
Veal	loin	well-done	low/medium	100°C/185°F	20-25
	leg	well-done	low/medium	100°C/185°F	20-25
	shoulder	well-done	low/medium	100°C/185°F	20-25
Poultry	chicken	well-done	low/medium	100°C/185°F	15-20
	turkey	well-done	low/medium	100°C/185°F	12-20*
	duckling	well-done	low/medium	100°C/185°F	15-20

*cooking times will vary considerably according to the weight of the bird ie. the larger and heavier the bird, the faster the cooking time.

Grilling

Food	Cut	Size or Weight	Heat Setting	Approximate Cooking Time (Each Side) In Minutes		
				Rare	Medium	Well-Done
Beef	steak	2.5cm (1 inch)	high	3-4	4-5	5-6
	steak	4cm (1½ inches)	high	5-6	7-8	9-10
	steak*	5cm (2 inches)	high	7-8	9-10	10-11
	flank steak	whole	high	3-4+		
	hamburger	2.5cm (1 inch)	medium/high	3-4	5-6	6-8
Lamb	chops	2.5cm (1 inch)	medium/high	5-6	7-8	9-10
	liver**	1cm (½ inch)	medium/high		5-6	
Pork	chops	2.5cm (1 inch)	medium/high			15-18
	spare ribs	whole or section	medium			55-75
	liver **	1cm (½ inch)	medium/high		6-7	
	ham	2.5cm (1 inch)	medium			15-20
Poultry	chicken	1.5kg (3½ lb) (split)	medium			35-45
	duck	1.75kg (4 lb) (split)	medium	5-6	10-12	25-28
Veal	steak or chops	2.5cm (1 inch)	medium			9-12
Fish	steak	1cm (½ inch)	medium			2-3
	steak	2.5cm (1 inch)	medium			5
	whole fish:	allow 10 minutes per 2.5cm (1 inch) of thickness eg. a fish 5cm (2 inches) thick will require 20 minutes cooking (10 minutes per side).				
Lobster split		500-750 g (1-1½ lb)	medium/high			7-10

*If the steak is 5cm (2 inches) or more thick you can use a meat thermometer to judge - steak is rare at 70°C/130°F, well-done at 90°C/170°F

+Maximum cooking time for the steak to remain tender.

**Avoid overcooking or the liver will become tough.

Spit-Roasting

Food	Cut	Size or Weight	Heat Setting	Approximate Cooking Time In hours*		
				Rare 75°C/140°F	Medium 85°C/160°F	Well-Done 90°C/170°F
Beef	rump	1.25-2.25kg (3-5 lb)	medium	1½-2	2¼-3	3-4
	sirloin	2.25-2.75kg (5-6 lb)	medium/high	1¼-1¾	2¼-3	3-4
	rolled rib	1.75-2.75kg (4-6 lb)	medium/high	2-2½	2¼-3	3¼-4
Lamb	leg rolled	1.5-3.5kg (3½-8 lb)	medium	1-1¼	1½-2	2-3¼
	shoulder	1.25-2.75kg (3-6 lb)	medium	1-1¼	1½-2	2-3¼
						100°C/185°F
Pork	shoulder	1.25-2.75kg (3-6 lb)	medium/high			2-3
	loin	1.25-2.25kg (3-5 lb)	medium/high			2-3
	spare ribs	1-1.75kg (2-4 lb)	medium/high			1-1¾
	fresh ham	2.25-3.5kg (5-8 lb)	medium			3½-4½
Poultry	chicken	1.1-2.25kg (2½-5 lb)	medium			1-1½
	turkey	3.5-7kg (8-16 lb)	medium			2-4
	duckling	1.75-2.75kg (4-6 lb)	medium			1-2
Veal	leg rolled	2.25-3.5kg (5-8 lb)	medium			2-3
	shoulder	1.25-2.25kg (3-5 lb)	medium			1½-2½
	loin	2.25-2.75kg (5-6 lb)	medium			1½-2¼
						65-70°C/ 120-130°F
Fish	large, whole	2.25-4.5kg (5-10 lb)	low/medium			1-1¼
	small, whole	750g-1.75kg (1½-4 lb)	low/medium			½-1

* For accuracy, use a meat thermometer and cook to the internal temperatures given in the chart on page opposite.

conversionchart

American and Australian Conversion Chart

Apart from the usual basic measures, such as 'teaspoon', 'tablespoon' and 'pinch', all the quantities and measurements in this book are given in both metric and imperial form. All spoon measures are level unless otherwise stated.

	BRITISH	AMERICAN	AUSTRALIAN
Teaspoons and tablespoons	1 teaspoon (5ml)	1 teaspoon (5ml)	1 teaspoon (5ml)
	1 tablespoon*	1 rounded tablespoon	1 scant tablespoon
	2 tablespoons	2 tablespoons	$1\frac{1}{2}$ tablespoons
	3 tablespoons	3 tablespoons	$2\frac{1}{2}$ tablespoons
	4 tablespoons	4 tablespoons	$3\frac{1}{2}$ tablespoons
	5 tablespoons	5 tablespoons	$4\frac{1}{2}$ tablespoons
Cup+ measures (liquid)	4 tablespoons	$\frac{1}{4}$ cup	$\frac{1}{4}$ cup
	125ml (4floz)	$\frac{1}{2}$ cup	$\frac{1}{2}$ cup
	250ml (8floz)	1 cup	1 cup
	450ml ($\frac{3}{4}$ pint)	2 cups	2 cups
	600ml (1 pint)	$2\frac{1}{2}$ cups	$2\frac{1}{2}$ cups
Cup measures (solid)	500g (1 lb) butter	2 cups	2 cups
	200g (7oz) long-grain rice	1 cup	1 cup
	500g (1 lb) granulated sugar	2 cups	2 cups
	50g (2oz) chopped onion	$\frac{1}{2}$ cup	$\frac{1}{2}$ cup
	50g (2oz) soft breadcrumbs	1 cup	1 cup
	125g (4oz) dry breadcrumbs	1 cup	1 cup
	500g (1 lb) plain flour	4 cups	4 cups
	50g (2oz) thinly sliced mushrooms	$\frac{1}{2}$ cup	$\frac{1}{2}$ cup
	125g (4oz) grated Cheddar cheese (lightly packed)	1 cup	1 cup
	125g (4oz) chopped nuts	1 cup	1 cup

*British standard tablespoon =15ml; American standard tablespoon =14.2ml; Australian standard tablespoon =20ml (Note: due to the nature of most of the recipes in this book, differences between tablespoon capacities should not have any adverse effect on the taste of the food.)

+American measuring cup = 250ml (8floz); Australian measuring cup = 250ml (8floz). (Note: British pint = 20floz; American pint = 16floz; Australian pint = 20floz)

International glossary
(just a few examples)
courgette	zucchini
sweet pepper	capsicum
aubergine	eggplant
mangetout	snow pea/sugar pea
crème fraiche	similar to double cream, but not so heavy in that it has a lower fat content (and fewer calories)

index

189

index

index